Early Praise for *From Ruby to Elixir*

Stephen's second book knocks it out of the park. Stephen is the ultimate Sherpa providing essential tools and sage advice to take the leap into a world of concurrency, simplicity, and power.

➤ **Amos King**
Founder, Binary Noggin

As a long-time Ruby developer, this book helped me quickly get up to speed when I joined an Elixir-based startup. It goes beyond syntax by teaching the philosophies that make the language a pleasure to work with. Consider this your invitation into the welcoming Elixir community.

➤ **Joe Chiarella**
Software Engineer, Adpipe

This book is the best introduction to Elixir that you can get and the last one you will need. It provides a firm grasp of the fundamentals and enough practical examples to get you started. It is the perfect guide for any developer who wants to switch from an object-oriented language to Elixir.

➤ **Peter Ullrich**
Founder, PCX IT

Even for someone without a specific background in Ruby, I have found this book extremely compelling and easy to follow. The examples and code still will make sense to those with a solid programming background, and it certainly will inspire you to check out Elixir further as it has for me.

➤ **Adam Haertter**
Configuration Developer, Donegal Insurance Group

From Ruby to Elixir

Unleash the Full Potential of Functional Programming

Stephen Bussey

The Pragmatic Bookshelf

Dallas, Texas

When we are aware that a term used in this book is claimed as a trademark, the designation is printed with an initial capital letter or in all capitals.

The Pragmatic Starter Kit, The Pragmatic Programmer, Pragmatic Programming, Pragmatic Bookshelf, PragProg and the linking *g* device are trademarks of The Pragmatic Programmers, LLC.

Every precaution was taken in the preparation of this book. However, the publisher assumes no responsibility for errors or omissions, or for damages that may result from the use of information (including program listings) contained herein.

For our complete catalog of hands-on, practical, and Pragmatic content for software developers, please visit *https://pragprog.com*.

The team that produced this book includes:

Publisher:	Dave Thomas
COO:	Janet Furlow
Executive Editor:	Susannah Davidson
Series Editor:	Sophie DeBenedetto
Development Editor:	Jacquelyn Carter
Copy Editor:	Corina Lebegioara
Indexing:	Potomac Indexing, LLC
Layout:	Gilson Graphics

For sales, volume licensing, and support, please contact *support@pragprog.com*.

For international rights, please contact *rights@pragprog.com*.

ISBN-13: 979-8-88865-031-8
Book version: P1.0—June 2024

Contents

Part II — Tools of the Trade

Acknowledgments

This is my second book, but it still took a village to create the best book possible. I truly appreciate the people who helped make this a reality. Their suggestions, feedback, and participation in the process are invaluable to me.

I love working with the staff at Pragmatic Bookshelf. Thank you Jackie Carter—the editor for this book—for all of the work that you did through the writing process. Your eye for what works well in a tech book tangibly improved every aspect of this book. Thanks to Sophie DeBenedetto—the Elixir series editor—for providing strategic advice at key times (especially when I became stuck!).

It takes a team of people to review a tech book. These people help validate the book's content, presentation style, pacing, structure, and more. Thank you to the following people for submitting technical reviews: Adam Haertter, Amos King, Brian Culler, Dan Dresselhaus, Dave Lively, De Wet Blomerus, Jess Burns, Joe Chiarella, Kurt Landrus, and Peter Ullrich. In addition, thanks to anyone who submitted an errata during the beta period.

This book covers powerful technology. The foundation is the Elixir programming language, so thank you to José Valim and the maintainers of Elixir. In addition, Ecto, Phoenix, Req, and Oban are all critical for the success of Elixir today and in the future. Thank you to the authors and maintainers of these libraries. Writing open-source software can be a thankless job, but your work is appreciated.

She is in the acknowledgments already, but a special thank you to my wife Jess. You are so supportive of my writing and every other crazy venture that I pursue. I'm able to do these things because of you.

Introduction

I have a confession about my journey into Elixir: it was a struggle. I could follow the guides and type out programs, but I didn't quite understand how everything fit together. Even though I was coming from Ruby, the topics were just not connecting. It wasn't until my third attempt that everything clicked.

I was missing the complete picture—the development of a real application combined with an understanding of the underlying concepts. Once I got it—it clicked quickly. I had an excellent mentor, Ben, who guided me throughout my journey.

Elixir has transformed the way that I think about, design, and code applications. The creators, community, and libraries empower me to think about code with a fresh perspective. My time with Elixir has been filled with enthusiasm, to say the least. My continued use of Elixir isn't only because it has one of the most high-tech runtimes, but also because it's simply more fun to use than other languages.

The goal of this book is to be your guide as you learn Elixir. The use of theory and practical examples will provide you with the full picture needed to succeed in your own journey—From Ruby to Elixir.

Who Should Read This Book?

This book is written for those coming from the Ruby programming language. If you're an intermediate-level Ruby programmer, then this book is perfect for you!

But this isn't the full picture! The Ruby examples in this book are likely to be relevant to any object-oriented programming language. There are some Ruby-specific comparisons, but the general approach still applies even if you're coming from Java, Python, C#, or others.

This book is ideal for those who have no Elixir knowledge or are at a beginner level. It's almost guaranteed that an Elixirist of any level will learn something new, but the majority of the content is about first steps with Elixir. In this book, you'll find Elixir code listings that walk you through theoretical examples and a practical application. We'll cover every example and project from start to finish, so you'll always know what to do next.

And if you're an experienced Elixirist reading this, maybe get a copy for your teammates.

About This Book

This book is organized into two parts. Part I is focused entirely on the fundamentals of the Elixir language. You'll learn how to read and write Elixir code during this part of the book, which will be necessary in Part II. We'll also cover slightly more advanced topics such as GenServer and the full power of pattern matching. Each section of Part I is designed to be completely standalone. The code examples are all chapter-specific, so you won't be in the dark if you decide to start out of order.

Part II is where theory meets practice. You'll write a real application that uses an API to send and receive text messages. The purpose of Part II is to introduce you to the best libraries in Elixir that are used to build robust applications. We'll cover database access, Phoenix web framework, a database-powered job system, and more. The examples in this part all build on the previous chapters, but you can start out of order with the provided code snapshots.

About the Code

Elixir is required for this book. Setup will depend on your operating system, but it's important that you're set up for success. I strongly recommend using the asdf[1] version manager to configure both Erlang and Elixir.

You'll learn about why you need different libraries in the first chapter, but it's important that you pick compatible versions of Elixir and Erlang. I recommend the versions found in Install Elixir on Your Computer, on page 10. There will be newer versions of these libraries by the time you're reading this book, so you may be able to substitute other versions. But always make sure that your Erlang version matches the OTP version of Elixir.

You'll also need to have Phoenix installed for the samples in this book. You can follow the HexDocs Installation guide[2] to get Phoenix set up. We'll cover this further at the appropriate time.

---

1. https://github.com/asdf-vm/asdf
2. https://hexdocs.pm/phoenix/installation.html

The Elixir snippets in this book aren't formatted according to the Mix formatter due to book formatting needs. You can use mix format to make sure that all snippets that you copy or hand-type are formatted properly.

You'll need to have PostgreSQL[3] installed for Part II. If you use Mac OS, then I recommend the postgres.app[4] installer to manage PostgreSQL.

Part II provides a mock SMS API application. This application simulates the Twilio SMS API, so you can use this book's code without setting up a real Twilio account. There will be instructions on how to set up the mock SMS API when it's time to do so.

Online Resources

The examples and source code shown in this book can be found under the source code link on the Pragmatic Bookshelf website.[5] You'll also find the sample application for Part II there.

Please report any errors or suggestions using the errata link that's available on the Pragmatic Bookshelf website.[6]

If you like this book and it serves you well, I hope that you'll let others know about it—your reviews really do help. Tweets and posts are a great way to help spread the word. You can find me on Twitter at @yoooodaaaa, or you can tweet @pragprog directly.

Stephen Bussey
May 2024

---

3. https://www.postgresql.org/download/
4. https://postgres.app
5. https://pragprog.com/titles/sbelixir/from-ruby-to-elixir
6. https://pragprog.com/titles/sbelixir/from-ruby-to-elixir

Part I

Fundamentals of Elixir

We'll start with the fundamentals of the Elixir language. You'll learn the core syntax of Elixir, the power of pattern matching, and what a GenServer is. We'll connect all of the material back to Ruby, so you'll have a familiar foundation to compare against.

## CHAPTER 1

Why Elixir? Why Now?

Elixir has emerged over the past few years as a "most loved" language[1] that's used by many businesses and hobbyists to write reliable software systems. Many Elixirists consider it their superpower of productivity and stability. Hopefully, by the end of this book, you'll see why this is the case.

It's hard to learn a new language, harder to become production-ready with it, and even harder still to convince your boss to actually let you use the new language in production. The juice is worth the squeeze, though. Elixir opens a new way of thinking about programming that carries over into other languages as well.

Your knowledge of Ruby influences how you view and write in other programming languages. Similarly, as you develop an understanding of Elixir, it will also influence how you think when writing code. Even if you were to never use Elixir in production, you'll still benefit and grow as a programmer.

We'll start this chapter by taking a look at what makes Ruby such a great language. You'll see why Elixir is a similarly great language and why its future is bright. You'll learn about the technology that Elixir is built on top of: Erlang, OTP, and the BEAM. Finally, you'll write a bit of Elixir code and run it on your computer.

Before we talk about Elixir, let's talk about Ruby.

The Joy of Ruby

Some people have pitted Elixir as being "against Ruby," but that's not the case. When you learn a new language, it doesn't have to come with a reduced respect for what you used in the past. It also doesn't mean that you can't use

---

1. https://survey.stackoverflow.co/2022/#technology-most-loved-dreaded-and-wanted

that language anymore. Especially with the rise of microservices, it's possible that you can program in Ruby and Elixir at the same company!

Ruby is a language founded with joy at its core, which leads to several non-technical aspects that make it an appealing language: a healthy foundational philosophy, a strong community, and continual improvement. Let's go over each point and how it benefits Ruby.

Solid Foundations

Yukihiro Matsumoto (Matz) created Ruby with a philosophy that programmers who use it should feel joy. To this day, his philosophy influences the design of the language, the way that libraries are built, and everything about Ruby.

The happiness of programmers is just as important as what those programmers create because happiness affects all aspects of one's life. Businesses benefit from this as well. A happy programmer is more likely to be happy with their job, stay with their company, and create a better product.

A Strong Community

Matz's philosophy is felt in the community and is captured in the phrase "Matz is nice, so we are nice" or MINSWAN.[2] The Ruby community is welcoming and helpful, which is critical for the adoption of a language over time. New developers won't want to learn a language if they are pushed away due to negativity.

Another strength of the Ruby community is a culture of testing. This might be obvious to people who have spent a lot of time with Ruby, but it's certainly not true in all language communities. Having a culture of testing creates better libraries and applications. This testing culture contributes to joy over time.

Continual Improvement

Ruby isn't a static language. The language doesn't push many breaking changes (this would certainly not elicit joy), but it has continued to evolve. Many smart people and companies deliver performance improvements, increased security, and even large projects like type checking.

Plus, Ruby's major libraries have continued to innovate over the years. Ruby on Rails 7[3] is the best release of Rails yet. It continues to set a high bar for programmer productivity and happiness.

---

2. https://en.wiktionary.org/wiki/MINASWAN
3. https://rubyonrails.org/

The continued improvements to Ruby guarantee relevance for Ruby developers. Ruby isn't going anywhere, and it isn't a goal of this book to try to replace Ruby with Elixir.

Next, let's explore a bit of what makes Elixir special.

The Case for Elixir

Anytime you pick a new technology, you'll have to make a case for it. The first consideration is your personal decision of whether you want to spend time learning the language. Next, you'll need to bring it to your professional peers and get their buy-in that they also want to spend time learning it. Finally, your business will need to make the case of whether they want to invest in it. Even if you're just a hobbyist who is curious about Elixir, you still need to justify learning it over other languages.

The technical aspects of a language are obviously important in these decisions, but the nontechnical aspects are just as important. In the previous section, we spent a lot of time talking about the nontechnical aspects that make Ruby a joy to use and learn.

We'll briefly cover a few nontechnical strengths of Elixir, but we'll also look at why the technology itself is appealing.

Nontechnical Strengths

Elixir is small and relatively new. These are two things that you'll be working against when you make the case for it. However, Elixir finds strength in its community, innovation, and philosophy.

Close-Knit Community
    The Elixir Forums[4] and Elixir Slack[5] are a wealth of knowledge and friendly faces. It's rare that a question goes unanswered in these places because the community shows up to help.

Culture of Testing
    Elixir, like Ruby, has a healthy testing culture that permeates every layer of the technical stack. It's rare to find untested libraries.

Language Design Philosophy
    Elixir doesn't have a vocalized philosophy like Ruby does, but it's clear that it's influenced by other languages. Elixir's creator, José Valim[6], has

---

4. https://elixirforum.com
5. https://elixir-slack.community/
6. https://twitter.com/josevalim

talked about being inspired by Ruby, Clojure, and Erlang. In fact, José was on the Rails Core Team, as well as the team that created the popular Devise library.

Elixir's language syntax is pleasant to use and elicits joy, much like Ruby's. For example, the Elixir core team works hard to avoid breaking changes—you can usually upgrade Elixir versions without too much work. That creates joy when upgrading from one version to another—an otherwise notoriously painful task.

Continual Innovation

Over the past few years, a ton of innovative features and libraries have been added to the Elixir ecosystem. These have been developed by the core team but also by private companies developing edge-pushing libraries.

The most well-known innovations in this space are Phoenix LiveView,[7] machine learning with Nx,[8] and hardware development with Nerves.[9]

A healthy foundation wouldn't matter if the technical aspects weren't also strong. Let's look at why Elixir is appealing for modern application development.

A Solid Foundation with the BEAM

Elixir is a functional programming language that's built on top of an almost forty-year-old foundation, the BEAM (Bogdan/Björn's Erlang Abstract Machine). We'll be going into what that is in the next section, but for now the important takeaway is that it's a unique runtime that empowers parallelism and fault tolerance in a way that isn't common in other languages.

The combination of fault tolerance and isolation is a premier strength of Elixir and the BEAM. Errors are going to happen, whether they are bugs, service outages, or anything in between. The BEAM provides ways for us to determine how errors should affect our application. Do you want an error to bring down the whole thing? Do you want an error to only affect the request that it was serving? Do you want to restart a piece of your system when an error occurs? Select the failure mode of your application so your application behaves predictably when things go wrong.

It's human nature to focus on the happy path. When evaluating a programming language, that would mean evaluating how you code in it, the libraries you use, and how data flows through your system. But the unhappy path is

---

7. https://github.com/phoenixframework/phoenix_live_view
8. https://github.com/elixir-nx
9. https://www.nerves-project.org/

just as (or sometimes more!) important. Elixir and the BEAM provide a core foundation for programming the unhappy path you want, rather than taking whatever you get.

Technical Benefits

Elixir applications can fully utilize their host CPU cores (parallelism) without having to write complex code. It's possible for other languages to achieve this same level of parallelism, but the unique aspect is how simple it is to achieve this with Elixir—it's nearly free.

It's easy to overlook the impact of this. If your web application is served on a 4-core server and you increase it to an 8-core server, you'll likely get twice the throughput out of it without making any changes. Despite it seeming like it should be common in other languages, it's not. Many languages (including Ruby) become bound as the server size grows, and applications can't utilize all of their cores when that happens.

Parallelism is crucial for modern programming, but the opposite of parallelism is just as important—serial code. Elixir provides excellent ways to control when code executes in parallel and when it executes serially.

The combination of parallel and serial code gives you complete control over your system runtime performance. This is unmatched in almost any other programming language today. Elixir (and BEAM languages) are equipped with these world-class capabilities out of the box.

Elixir is well-suited for building reliable, modern systems. This especially applies to web systems, but Elixir can be used in hardware systems, communication systems, machine learning, and more. You'll write more performant systems that are cheaper to run when you use Elixir.

These are only a few of the technical benefits of Elixir. A lot of Elixir's greatest strengths come from its foundation with Erlang and the BEAM. Let's dive into what those are next.

Erlang, OTP, Elixir, and Friends

Elixir stands on the shoulders of giants that have been around for decades, like Erlang, OTP, and the BEAM. You can be confident that Elixir's runtime is world-class, even though it's new when compared to other languages.

You don't have to know a ton about Erlang, OTP, and the BEAM to use Elixir, but you'll run into the edges of them at some point. For example, when installing Elixir you also had to ensure that the proper Erlang version was installed.

We'll cover all of these terms so that you understand what each is, how they differ from each other, and how you'll interact with each over time. We're going to start at the top and work our way down, with Elixir first.

Elixir Builds on Erlang

Elixir[10] is a functional programming language that was first released in 2012. It places an emphasis on expressive syntax that conveys the meaning of code quickly.

Elixir is a compiled language. This means that the code you write will be transformed into "something else" before it runs. Ruby, on the other hand, is an interpreted language, which means that source code is directly executed by a Ruby interpreter. The Ruby interpreter might still make optimizations to your code—like apply JIT optimizations to your code—but you can save a Ruby file and run it as is.

You'll write Elixir code when you work on your app, but it's compiled into a totally different programming language called Erlang. This seems confusing at first, but it's not magic. The Elixir compiler runs a few passes over your code to turn it into Erlang code. This Erlang code gets compiled into .beam files that are executed by the BEAM virtual machine. You'll likely never have to worry about this unless you have very advanced deployment needs.

Due to this compilation strategy, Elixir and Erlang code can be used in the same application. You wouldn't normally do this yourself, but you'll definitely use libraries in your Elixir application that are written in Erlang. And you likely won't even know unless you look at a library's source code.

A lot of things in the Elixir ecosystem are directly built on top of what Erlang provides. Let's look at Erlang and its set of libraries called OTP.

Erlang/OTP

Erlang[11] is a functional programming language that was first released in 1998. It started its journey as a closed-source language developed in 1986 by the telecommunications company Ericsson. As such, it was designed for the challenges of telecommunications. Parallelism, fault isolation, and data isolation were built into the language runtime instead of being tacked on later.

Erlang is a programming language, but its core set of libraries is separate from it. These libraries are referred to as OTP, an acronym for Open Telecom Platform.

---

10. https://elixir-lang.org/
11. https://www.erlang.org/

This often confuses many new Elixir developers. OTP does have "Telecom" in the name, but it has nothing to do with phone systems. It's simply a relic of the development history of Erlang and its corporate relationship with Ericsson.

OTP consists of Erlang libraries, the Erlang runtime system, ready-to-use components, and a set of design principles that can be followed by Erlang programs. While OTP is technically separate from Erlang, in practice they are always shipped as a unit. When you download Erlang, you'll download a package called "Erlang/OTP" which includes both the Erlang language and the OTP libraries.

The BEAM

Erlang, Elixir, and OTP don't really do much by themselves. They need a runtime to execute on top of. This is where the BEAM comes in. BEAM stands for "Bogdan/Björn's Erlang Abstract Machine," but everyone simply calls it "the BEAM."

We'll be taking a look at parallelism in Chapter 5, GenServers: Build Cities, Not Skyscrapers, on page 65, but the important thing for now is that the BEAM natively supports the primitives that allow Elixir to work like it does. If you took Elixir code and tried to run it on a runtime that didn't work the same way, a lot of the strengths would weaken or even disappear. The combination of Elixir and the BEAM is what makes it world-class.

The BEAM has evolved and changed over time. Its name has also changed, so who knows if we'll see a totally different iteration of it at some point in the future! There's an excellent timeline[12] that goes over the history of Erlang and the various runtimes. This may not be interesting to everyone, but it's a fascinating collection of the evolution of Erlang over time.

Put It All Together

It seems like a lot, but you need to know only a few things to get started:

- Elixir is the programming language that you'll directly work with.

- Erlang is a language that you likely won't need to worry about.

- OTP is a set of libraries that Elixir uses to provide critical concepts and features.

- The BEAM is what runs your code.

---

12. https://www.erlang.org/blog/beam-compiler-history/

The most complicated time that requires explicit control over Elixir, Erlang, and the BEAM is during installation. Unfortunately, this is also the first experience you'll have! So let's specifically cover best practices for installation.

Install Elixir on Your Computer

When you install Elixir on your computer, you *must* properly install the right Erlang/OTP versions or you could run into frustrating errors. You should always specify versions of each so that everything works as you expect it to. This is because Elixir frequently calls OTP functions, which rely on having the correct version installed.

If you don't know where to get started, just pick the latest version for each. Things might slightly change over time, but you can always adapt or combine different versions as needed.

I recommend the asdf[13] version manager with plugins for asdf-elixir[14] and asdf-erlang.[15] These plugins do a good job at managing the installation needs of compiling Erlang/OTP over time, so you're most likely to succeed with them. You can find online guides[16] that walk you through how to set up asdf.

You can use asdf in a few ways, but you'll have the most success if you create a .tool-versions file in your project root and commit it to version control. Here's an example of that file with the tool versions used during the production of this book:

```
.tool-versions
elixir 1.16.0-otp-26
erlang 26.2.1
```

Once you have asdf installed—along with the Elixir and Erlang plugins—you can run asdf install in the directory with this file, and it will install the correct versions.

Notice that the Elixir version uses the -otp suffix. This tells asdf to install the Elixir version that has been compiled with a specific Erlang/OTP version.

The .tool-versions file allows your entire team to have the same version of Elixir and Erlang/OTP. This also makes it clear which versions are required when you deploy code to production.

---

13. https://github.com/asdf-vm/asdf
14. https://github.com/asdf-vm/asdf-elixir
15. https://github.com/asdf-vm/asdf-erlang
16. https://thinkingelixir.com/install-elixir-using-asdf/

I don't suggest using brew install elixir or other global package managers. There's too much that inevitably goes wrong. This is especially true if you're working on multiple projects that may update at different times.

Before we wrap up this chapter, let's write a bit of code!

Write Your First Elixir Code

While Elixir is a compiled language, it has an interactive console that makes it easy to quickly experiment with code. We'll use Elixir's console—IEx—to write and execute basic code. IEx (Interactive Elixir) is the equivalent of IRB (Interactive Ruby) in the Ruby world.

IEx is commonly used to quickly prototype code locally, although it's a bit more powerful than that. One of the convenient techniques that you can use—and you will later in the book—is to run your web server and interactive console at the same time. This allows you to directly experiment with and modify a running application.

It's easy to start an IEx session. Run the following command on your command line. If you see an error, then go back to the previous section and make sure that Elixir and Erlang/OTP are properly installed.

```
$ iex
Erlang/OTP 24 [erts-12.0.3]...

Interactive Elixir (1.12.3) - press Ctrl+C to exit (type h() ENTER for help)
iex(1)>
```

Enter a few lines of code to see things working:

```
iex(1)> 1 + 1
2
iex(2)> IO.puts("A string")
A string
:ok
iex(3)> adder = fn (a, b) -> a + b end
#Function<43.40011524/2 in :erl_eval.expr/5>
iex(4)> adder.(17, 25)
42
```

When you're done, hit Ctrl + C, followed by A, and then ENTER. This is the easiest way to exit out of the IEx session.

Okay, I'll admit this isn't *that* exciting yet. But you have written your first lines of Elixir! As you enter each line, IEx evaluates it, executes it, and outputs the result on the next line—just like IRB does.

This example demonstrates two different types of functions. The first is a module-based function (IO.puts/1) and the second is an anonymous function that we've assigned to the adder variable.

This looks a bit foreign right now, but the next chapter will clear it all up!

Wrapping Up

Ruby is a language with joy at its core. The philosophy that pins the foundation of the language's design also drives the community and culture that has evolved around Ruby. This has allowed Ruby to remain relevant and continually evolve over the years. It has been and remains a great language.

When looking for a new language, these qualities shouldn't be sacrificed: joy, pragmatism, healthy community, and continual innovation. Elixir delivers on these qualities, and it has emerged into a language loved by many. Deciding to learn a new language is a big decision, but Elixir is worth the effort.

Elixir provides a world-class technical foundation for all types of applications. Web development is a primary use case, but hardware and machine learning are also handled really well. Elixir's focus on easy parallelism and fault tolerance gives it a huge advantage over other languages.

Elixir doesn't exist by itself—it stands on the shoulders of giants that have been in development for decades. Erlang, OTP, and the BEAM help Elixir deliver a world-class development and production experience. But it's done in such a way that you don't need to worry about the foundations that it's built on. You can write and ship Elixir but still benefit from the rock-solid BEAM runtime.

You wrote some of your first lines of Elixir code in this chapter. In the next chapter, we'll dive deeper into the Elixir language. You'll learn about basic syntax, modules, functions, lists, and structs. Along the way, these concepts will be compared to equivalent concepts in Ruby. Let's get to it!

## CHAPTER 2

New Language, New Syntax

The first look at a new language is a daunting task. Symbols look foreign, and you're trying to understand how everything fits together. It's the same for all languages, and Elixir is no different. But Elixir has a fairly small amount of syntax, which makes it relatively quick to learn.

Elixir has three distinct parts that you'll need to be comfortable with before you are ready to build applications. The first, and most basic, is the syntax of Elixir. Next is the process model and how to leverage OTP. And finally, you'll need to know about the common libraries that you'll use when you write applications. We'll cover all of these topics throughout this book, but this chapter focuses on Elixir's syntax.

The goal is that, by the end of Part I, you'll be able to read everyday Elixir code without fear, although you won't have yet put it together into an application. Don't worry, we'll write an application in Part II. You'll see comparisons made with Ruby along the way. This will help you more quickly turn your Ruby knowledge into Elixir experience.

In this chapter, we'll go over data types, operators, modules, and functions. You'll see how these things fit together to create the foundations of Elixir applications. And you'll see where danger can lurk in some of the syntaxes. But first, let's step back and take a look at some differences between Elixir and Ruby.

The Big Picture

On the surface, Ruby and Elixir code appear very similar to each other, but make no mistake, they are quite different. It's best to acknowledge their visual similarities, but don't dwell on it or get frustrated that things work differently between them.

The most foundational difference between the languages is that Ruby is object-oriented while Elixir is function-oriented. Objects combine data and methods (functions) into a single instance, and objects interact with each other to form your application. Elixir has no objects, so functions must be provided the data that they operate on. You'll see Elixir patterns and concepts that feel a bit like objects, but don't be tricked—Elixir doesn't have objects.

Elixir has fewer features compared to Ruby. Because there are no objects, there is no inheritance. Additionally, data like integers, strings, and maps cannot be directly extended with helper methods. This can create the feeling of "how can I build the same app with fewer features at my disposal?" Don't worry, Elixir has everything you need to write great software.

Another big difference between Ruby and Elixir is data mutability. This refers to whether or not data can be directly modified after it's created. A simple demonstration of this is with a list of [1, 2, 3]. In Ruby, you can call list.pop and you'll receive the result (3). But the underlying data in list changes to [1, 2]. In Elixir, you can call List.pop_at(list, -1) and you'll receive both the result and the new list. The data in list remains the same.

There isn't an objectively right answer to which of these designs is better. But many people, including myself, prefer Elixir's immutable data and functional nature because it increases predictability and readability.

These are just some of the major differences between the languages. There are many more, ranging from the typical program's structure to the way that code executes. You'll undoubtedly see and make comparisons between the two as you learn Elixir. This is a good thing because you'll more quickly grasp concepts, but don't try to turn Elixir into Ruby, or vice-versa.

With that out of the way, let's look more closely at Elixir! We'll start with data types.

Data Types

Elixir has a simple set of data types—the usual suspects are all here. You use these types to store your application data and pass it as arguments to functions.

Ruby differs a bit in what you can do with basic data types. Everything in Ruby (including basic data types) is an object, so you can add methods to the object class in order to extend the data type. For example, Ruby on Rails has implemented methods to make syntax like 10.days.from_now possible. This works because ActiveSupport has extended the Integer class with these methods.

The design of Ruby's object extension is elegant, but you won't find it in Elixir. This isn't necessarily a bad thing though. Functions in Elixir are explicitly invoked with the module name—more on this later—so you know exactly where a function is defined, and you can quickly find its documentation or source code. Every design decision has trade-offs, and Elixir's function-oriented approach trades elegance for explicitness.

Let's quickly go over Elixir's data types. These aren't all of them, but they are the most common ones you'll use. Some are simple, but others require a bit more explanation:

Atom

Atoms are named constants expressed with a colon (:an_atom). They are like symbols in Ruby.

Boolean

Booleans are special atoms that represent truth (true or false).

Nil

nil is a special atom that represents the absence of a value.

Integer

Integers are expressed with digits (123) or via alternative base representations (0xA). You can add _ to integers to visually break up large numbers (1_000_000). Integers don't have a maximum size.

Float

Floats are expressed using digits and a period (10.53). They can also be expressed in scientific notation (1.0e10). Floats have a maximum size of 1.7976931348623157e+308.

Bitstring, Binary

Bitstrings represent a collection of bits. They are expressed using angle brackets (<<1, 2>>). Binaries are a type of bitstring with a number of bits divisible by 8. The most common type of binary is a string. Bitstrings can be slightly jarring to see in real-world code—because they're not common in other languages—but they allow for easy interaction with binary data.

String

Strings are expressed using double quotations, like "Hello!". Strings are easy to work with, as in Ruby, but are actually stored as binary bitstrings under the hood. In practice you won't have to worry about this, but sometimes you'll see function calls like is_binary(var), which is commonly used to check for a string argument.

A common mistake is to use single quotations ('Hello!') to express a string. This often ends with confusion and frustration because "hello" != 'hello'. Single quotation marks are used to represent Erlang's version of a string (charlist) and are really only used in Elixir code that directly interacts with Erlang code.

List

Lists are expressed using brackets—[1, 2, 3]. The next chapter has a section dedicated to them.

Tuple

Tuples are fixed-size lists that are expressed using braces—{1, 2, 3}. The differences between tuples and lists are covered in the next chapter.

Map

Maps are key-value dictionaries expressed with percent-brace—%{a: "map"}. They also appear in the next chapter.

We'll dig deeper into several of these data types throughout the chapter. First, let's go over the operators that are built into Elixir.

Operators

Elixir comes with a set of basic operators that largely work the way that you would expect. Most operators will feel similar to the operators you use in Ruby, and you'll be right at home. But a few of these operators will behave much differently than similar operators in Ruby.

We'll cover the most commonly used Elixir operators, and you'll see the important differences that a few of these operators have compared to Ruby.

Assignment (Match)

= is called the match operator. You can use this as you would in Ruby (my_var = 1), but it does much more than just assignment.

It's also used for pattern matching and complex structural comparisons ([a, b] = [1, 2]). Pattern matching is one of the most important parts of Elixir's syntax, so Chapter 4, Pattern Matching Your Way to Success, on page 49 is dedicated to it.

Comparison

Elixir provides ==, !=, >, >=, <, <=, ===, !== operators. These largely work as you would expect, with a couple of twists.

=== and !== are more strict versions of the two-character counterparts (1 !== 1.0 but 1 == 1.0). The three-character comparison operators are not commonly seen in Elixir codebases.

Comparison can be done on any data type ("hi" > 3). This might cause some head-scratching at first, but it simplifies the implementation of data comparison and makes it easier to write sorting functions.

Arithmetic

+, -, *, / are the built-in arithmetic operators. Other math operators (modulo, power, rounding) are implemented in the Integer and Float modules.

Boolean Operators

There are two flavors of boolean operators, just as in Ruby. and, or, and not are strict boolean operators. &&, ||, and ! are truthy boolean operators.

Strict boolean operators expect the first argument to be a boolean. Truthy boolean operators work on any data type. So, 1 && true is valid but 1 and true throws an error. Truthy boolean operators are more commonly used than strict boolean operators.

In Ruby, and has a different precedence than &&. This leads to subtle bugs in certain situations. This isn't the case in Elixir because and and && have the same precedence.

Throw and Raise

Elixir supports throw and raise operators to bubble exceptions through the stack. throw can be used to propagate any Elixir term, but raise is only for Elixir exceptions. In practice, these aren't used often. Most Elixirists prefer to use pattern matching to handle errors in their application. (You'll learn about this in Chapter 4, Pattern Matching Your Way to Success, on page 49.)

Function Piping

The pipe operator |> is heavily used by Elixir programmers. This operator takes a value and passes it as the first argument to a provided function. You use this to create a chain of function calls that's easily readable and well-formatted. Each return value is then piped into the next function. This is similar to method chaining in Ruby.

```
"a string"
|> String.upcase()
|> String.replace("A", "THE")

# "THE STRING"
```

Without using function piping, this would be equivalent to:

```
String.replace(String.upcase("a string"), "A", "THE")
```

You'll encounter other operators and data types as you learn Elixir, but this covers the majority of what you'll use day-to-day. We'll cover a few other operators (such as string concatenation and combining lists) in Chapter 4, Pattern Matching Your Way to Success, on page 49.

If you run into something you don't understand, review the Kernel module documentation.[1] It has information about types, operators, and additional best practice considerations.

The Kernel Module

Elixir operators are either implemented by the compiler or in a special module called Kernel. The Kernel module is automatically available to all Elixir code, so you never have to think about it.

Elixir, unlike Ruby, doesn't let you extend modules like Kernel. So you can't automatically include functions in all modules.

Now, let's move on to modules and functions.

Module and Function Basics

Elixir is a functional language, so—as you would expect—the work of an Elixir application is done in functions. Functions take input data, process it according to the function's code, and then return a result. Modules are containers of functions that you have grouped together. They are mainly used as an organizational tool.

We are talking about modules and functions at the same time because they go hand-in-hand with each other. A module doesn't serve a purpose without functions, and functions need a module to exist in.

The main purpose of modules is to hold functions, but they actually do more than this. Later in this chapter, we'll look at additional syntax that's available to modules.

We'll cover two types of functions in this chapter: named functions and anonymous functions. Named functions are the most commonly used functions in an Elixir app (over 90% of a typical Elixir app). Especially as you start out, lean toward using named functions instead of anonymous functions.

---

1. https://hexdocs.pm/elixir/1.14/Kernel.html

As you read this section, you'll likely make comparisons to Ruby modules and classes. Elixir modules are similar to Ruby modules because they each serve the purpose of organization. However, Elixir modules offer hook points that can be used for metaprogramming. This makes them similar to classes as well. It's best to acknowledge the similarities in name and syntax but accept that Ruby and Elixir have their differences.

Before we write a module, we need an easier way to run our code. Manually typing code into an IEx session is a bit cumbersome. Luckily, Elixir has Mix.

Mix Projects

Mix[2] is a tool that helps us create, manage, compile, and deploy Elixir applications. Plus, it manages our dependencies for us too! It ships with Elixir, so you already have it available. It's similar to Ruby's Rake tool combined with Bundler.

You could compile and execute Elixir files yourself, but it would be a pretty messy process. You would need to worry about dependencies, loading the compiled files, and then executing a script. Mix handles all of this for us. An application that uses Mix is referred to as a Mix project.

The next few chapters use a Mix project to compile longer sections of code. You're going to create that project now, but make sure to put it in a convenient directory because you'll be coming back to it several times.

Run the following command in a directory that you want to create the Mix project in:

```
$ mix new examples
$ cd examples
$ mix test
```

Nice! You just made a new Mix project called examples. This will allow you to easily run the scripts in this chapter. If you saw green when you ran mix test, then everything is set up properly. If you see red, then check to make sure that your Elixir and Erlang versions are installed correctly.

Inside of the newly created examples directory, you'll see lib and test folders. Application code goes into the lib folder and tests go into the test folder. Technically, you could implement a different code organization, but it's extremely rare to see any other type of code structure in Elixir applications.

Now we can write some Elixir!

---

2.   https://hexdocs.pm/mix/Mix.html

Create a Module

You're ready to write code in your Mix project. We'll start with a simple module containing a few functions. Create the following file in lib/examples/modules/one.ex:

```
elixir_examples/lib/examples/modules/one.ex
defmodule Examples.Modules.One do
  def hello do
    :world
  end

  def welcome(name) do
    "Welcome #{name}"
  end
end
```

The code inside of the defmodule block becomes the module once Elixir compiles it. defmodule is a special type of syntax called a macro.

Similarly, def is a macro that defines a function. Functions can have arguments (like welcome/1 does) or they can exclude arguments (like hello/0).

These functions are inside of a module and are named, so we call them named functions. We refer to named functions with the syntax Module.function/arity, like Examples.Modules.One.welcome/1. (Arity refers to the number of arguments passed into a function.) Sometimes the module name is excluded if it's referring to the current module that you're in.

Macros: With Power Comes Responsibility

The best advice about macros is "don't write macros," as Chris McCord wrote in *Metaprogramming Elixir [McC15]*.

This is slightly sarcastic advice, but it highlights the fact macros can be tricky to write. Especially when you're first starting out.

Macros are functions that emit code when compiled. Macros let you quickly integrate complex libraries or functions into your code. They are most often used by library authors or by developers who are creating an abstraction. This is referred to as metaprogramming.

We won't cover macros in depth in this book, although they will pop up occasionally. Chris McCord's book is my go-to resource for macros, and the official documentation is also very good.

It's not required to make your module names match the file name, but the convention is to do so because it helps with organization. Every .ex file inside of your lib folder will be available to your application when you run it. You're probably used to Ruby's auto-loading gem—Zeitwerk—but Mix handles all of this for us.

Let's execute the functions by loading a Mix-enabled IEx session. You do this by passing the -S mix flag to iex:

```
$ iex -S mix
Compiling 2 files (.ex)
iex(1)> Examples.Modules.One.hello()
:world

iex(2)> Examples.Modules.One.welcome("Steve")
"Welcome Steve"

iex(3)> Examples.Modules.One.welcome()
** (UndefinedFunctionError) function Examples.Modules.One.welcome/0
   is undefined or private. Did you mean one of:

     * welcome/1

   (examples 0.1.0) Examples.Modules.One.welcome()
```

You can easily invoke the functions defined in your module, but giving a name that doesn't exist or an incorrect number of arguments will result in an error.

Take a look at comparable code in Ruby. It's very similar, but there are significant differences:

```
ruby_examples/one.rb
class One
  def hello
    :world
  end

  def welcome(name)
    "Welcome #{name}"
  end
end

one = One.new
one.hello #> :world
one.welcome("You") #> "Welcome You"
```

Ruby methods can be class-level or object-level, and classes can be instantiated as object instances. Remember that Elixir has no objects, only functions.

This section covered one type of function (named functions), but there's another type of function that's used in different scenarios. Let's take a look at anonymous functions next.

Fun with Functions

Functions are simple at first glance—they have a name, arguments, and a body. But Elixir allows you to overload functions in several different ways that aren't possible in most other languages. Even though they are simple, this ability to overload them makes functions very powerful.

You wrote named functions in the previous section. In this section, you'll deal with anonymous functions. Anonymous functions are a quick and convenient way to define functions inline in your code.

Let's get started with anonymous functions.

Anonymous Functions

Anonymous functions are ones that have no name. They are commonly used when passing behavior into a different function, such as an enumeration function.

Anonymous functions are quick and easy to define, and they keep behavior directly next to the call site. These attributes make them convenient to write and easy to read. However, the biggest benefit of them is that scoping is maintained. All of the variables that are in-scope where the anonymous function is defined can be used by the anonymous function.

Here's an example of anonymous functions. Type the following into IEx:

```
$ iex
iex(1)> Enum.map([1, 2, 3], fn num -> num * 2 end)
[2, 4, 6]

iex(2)> iterate = fn num -> num * 2 end
#Function<44.40011524/1 in :erl_eval.expr/5>

iex(3)> Enum.map([1, 2, 3], iterate)
[2, 4, 6]

iex(4)> iterate.(2)
4
```

Anonymous functions are similar to Procs in Ruby. Let's look at Ruby code that uses Procs to enumerate over an array.

```
$ irb
irb(main)> [1, 2, 3].map { |num| num * 2 }
=> [2, 4, 6]

irb(main)> iterate = ->(num) { num * 2 }
=> #<Proc:0x000000014422e918 (irb):1 (lambda)>
```

```
irb(main)> [1, 2, 3].map(&iterate)
=> [2, 4, 6]
irb(main)> iterate.(2)
4
```

Ruby Procs can be assigned to variables and passed around or can be defined inline and used only by a single method. This is exactly how anonymous functions in Elixir work.

Anonymous functions can be defined across multiple lines (similar to Ruby Procs) or can be defined on a single line. You must put a period character between the variable name and the function arguments when you invoke an anonymous function, like my_function.(my_argument).

A major similarity between Ruby and Elixir is that the last statement executed by a function is returned. There is no explicit return syntax in Elixir. Instead, you use conditionals and pattern matching to structure your functions so the intended value is returned. This becomes fairly natural as you get the hang of Elixir.

Next, let's look at how functions can be overloaded.

Overloading Your Functions

An overloaded function is a function that has multiple entry points based on the input arguments. Some languages limit function overloading to the number of arguments—my_func/0 and my_func/1 would be considered overloaded. But Elixir goes beyond this.

In Elixir, you can overload the same function based on the argument data itself. So, my_func("hello") could have a different function body than my_func("hola").

Let's write an overloaded function in Elixir. Create lib/examples/modules/two.ex and add the following code:

elixir_examples/lib/examples/modules/two.ex
```
defmodule Examples.Modules.Two do
  def hello do
    "Hello"
  end

  # This is a reference to Erlang: The Movie
  def hello("Mike") do
    "Hello Mike, Hello Joe"
  end

  def hello(name) do
    "Hello #{name}"
  end
```

```
  def hi(name \\ "Reader") do
    "Hi #{name}"
  end
end
```

This code also demonstrates that Elixir supports default function arguments using the \\ operator. This creates two versions of our function—hi/0 and hi/1—that have different values for the name argument.

When you run this in IEx, you'll see that our functions behave differently based on the number of arguments and the data in those arguments:

```
$ iex -S mix

iex> Examples.Modules.Two.hello()
"Hello"

iex> Examples.Modules.Two.hello("Steve")
"Hello Steve"

iex> Examples.Modules.Two.hello("Mike")
"Hello Mike, Hello Joe"

iex> Examples.Modules.Two.hi()
"Hi Reader"

iex> Examples.Modules.Two.hi("Steve")
"Hi Steve"
```

This technique may be completely new to you because Ruby doesn't have method overloading. If you define a Ruby method with the same name as a previously defined method, then the old definition will be skipped. For example, the following Ruby method returns "hello":

```
ruby_examples/two.rb
class Overload
  def hello(name)
    "Hi #{name}"
  end

  def hello
    "hello"
  end
end

Overload.new.hello #> "hello"
Overload.new.hello("Steve") #> ArgumentError (given 1, expected 0)
```

Even if the Ruby method was defined with a different number of arguments, there would still be only one version of that method. You would need to implement a different behavior in the body of the method instead of having multiple definitions.

Overloaded functions are extremely common in Elixir applications. They are regularly used for recursive functions and for changing behavior based on configuration. You'll see more examples of overloading throughout Part I.

Up next, we're going to take a look at a convenient shorthand to create anonymous functions.

Capturing Functions

Anonymous functions are created using the fn keyword. But there's another technique to create anonymous functions called function capturing. This technique lets you define an anonymous function with a short syntax. It's very popular when defining a one- or two-line function for use in modules like Enum.

We'll go over the syntax for function capturing as well as how it can be used on named functions. It's a quick bit of syntax, so let's dive right in!

Capturing Anonymous Functions

Captured functions begin with the & symbol. Inside the body of the function, &1 is used to refer to the first argument. Here's an example:

```
$ iex
iex(1)> Enum.map([1, 2, 3], & &1 * 2)
[2, 4, 6]
```

The phrase & &1 * 2 is a captured function. It's equivalent to fn x -> x * 2 end. For each enumeration of our list, the argument is passed into &1 and then multiplied by 2.

Captured functions can reference multiple arguments. In the previous example, Enum.map/2 calls a function that accepts a single argument. But a function like Enum.reduce/2 calls a function that accepts two arguments. If we wanted to use this in an anonymous function, it would look like this:

```
iex(2)> Enum.reduce([1, 2, 3], 0, & &1 + &2)
6
```

It's fairly rare to see a captured function that uses &2 or even &3. It just becomes too difficult to follow along with. In these cases, it's better to use fn to define the anonymous function.

The captured function syntax is a bit daunting at first, but it's a convenient way to define simple functions that span a single line. Many Elixir developers prefer this syntax for short iteration functions.

Function capturing has multiple use cases. Let's look at how it can be used to reference a named function.

Capturing Named Functions

You just saw how you can create a new anonymous function using the & operator. But we can use this same technique to capture a named function. Capturing a named function lets us treat it like an anonymous function.

Named functions in Elixir are referred to by Module.name/arity. This same format is used to capture a named function. For example, the code my_fn = & IO.puts/1 assigns the IO.puts/1 function to the my_fn variable. You could then call it using my_fn.("hi"). Let's see this in action. The next example captures the IO.puts/1 function and uses it in an enumerator over a list:

```
$ iex
iex(1)> Enum.each([1, 2], & IO.puts/1)
1
2
:ok
```

Capturing is also possible in Ruby, but it looks slightly different because you use the method method:

```
$ irb
irb(main)> [1,2].each(&method(:puts))
1
2
=> [1, 2]
```

Elixir's function capturing helps you keep your code clean. If you have multi-line anonymous functions, it's often better to create a named function and use function capturing to reference it.

Let's go over an example of extracting an anonymous function into a named one. The following code has inline/0 and extracted/0 functions. inline/0 passes a multi-line anonymous function as an argument to Enum.each/2. But extracted/0 captures the print_name/1 function and passes that into Enum.each/2 instead.

```
elixir_examples/lib/examples/modules/extract.ex
defmodule Examples.Modules.Extract do
  def inline do
    Enum.each(names(), fn name ->
      capitalized = String.capitalize(name)
      phrase = "Hello, #{capitalized}"
      IO.puts(phrase)
    end)
  end
```

```
def extracted do
  Enum.each(names(), & print_name/1)
end

defp print_name(name) do
  capitalized = String.capitalize(name)
  phrase = "Hello, #{capitalized}"
  IO.puts(phrase)
end

defp names do
  ["joe", "robert", "mike"]
end
end
```

These functions are identical in behavior, but the extracted function is easier to understand when read in isolation. This is a personal preference, but the Elixir community generally leans toward extracting multi-line functions.

Now that you've seen how to put functions together, let's go back to modules and look at some of the more advanced convenience-oriented concepts.

Advanced Module Keywords

You won't get too far into an Elixir application without seeing one of the following keywords: alias, require, import, or use. They all serve different purposes and are extensively used in Elixir modules. We'll go over each of them, including when you would use each.

Each of these module keywords can be used as many times as you want in a module. For example, you could alias two modules, require another, and use three more.

This section uses examples that won't actually compile, so you don't need to type them out. They're here to illustrate how the various keywords are used.

Alias

As you create your application, you will have long module names like MyApp.Widgets.Query.WidgetStore. Long module names allow you to cleanly name-space your application, but they are cumbersome to type everywhere. The alias keyword allows you to refer to a module using its shorter name.

```
defmodule ExampleModule do
  alias MyApp.Widgets.Query.WidgetStore
  alias MyApp.Widgets.Workers.WidgetSync
```

```
  def save_widget!(params) do
    widget = WidgetStore.create_widget!(params)
    WidgetSync.enqueue!(widget)
  end
end
```

The alias keyword refers to the provided module name using the last part of its name. So in this example, you can write WidgetStore instead of the fully qualified name.

You can specify multiple modules at once by using the syntax alias ParentModule.{First, Second}. This syntax has mixed reviews in the community—many people prefer to write each alias on its own line.

Import

The import keyword scopes a module's public functions into the current module. The function effectively becomes local to your module at that point. A common example of this is the Ecto.Changeset module:

```
defmodule ExampleModule do
  import Ecto.Changeset

  def changeset(attrs) do
    %MySchema{}
    |> cast(attrs, [:field])
    |> validate_required([:field])
  end
end
```

In this example, cast/3 and validate_required/2 are functions defined in the Ecto.Changeset module. (The arity may be higher than you are expecting. Remember that the pipe operator provides the first argument.)

To keep our code clean, we import the Ecto.Changeset module's functions and then use them directly. This syntax is most useful for a domain-specific language (DSL). It's common in Ecto primarily because Ecto is a DSL over database operations. We'll be using Ecto in Chapter 6, Persisting Data with Ecto, on page 87.

Require

If you want to use a macro function in your module, then you must require the module before you do so. If you forget to require the macro's module first, Elixir will give you a helpful warning.

The following code uses the Integer.is_even/1 macro, so the require Integer must be added to the module:

```
defmodule ExampleModule do
  require Integer

  def print_when_even(number) do
    if Integer.is_even(number) do
      IO.puts "It's even!"
    end
  end
end
```

If you try to use Integer.is_even/1 without requiring it, you'll get an error.

```
** (CompileError) you must require Integer before invoking
     the macro Integer.is_even/1
```

Use

The use keyword serves as a hook point during the compilation of a module. The module that's "used" will be able to add code to the module with the use statement. There is no like-for-like comparison with Ruby because Elixir's use is executed at compile time, but it's most similar to how ActiveSupport::Concern works.

use is often used by some libraries to create a seamless developer experience. The next example shows what an Ecto Schema looks like. This example shows several functions that make up a schema-building DSL:

```
defmodule SmsMessage do
  use Ecto.Schema

  schema "sms_messages" do
    field :body, :string
    field :from, :string
    field :to, :string
  end
end
```

The schema/2 and field/3 functions are all defined in the Ecto.Schema module. The line use Ecto.Schema makes these functions available inside of the module. A lot of complex setup is involved in pulling this off, so import won't work here.

To truly understand use, you have to understand that Elixir is a compiled language. Let's dive into what this means.

Compile Time vs. Runtime

Elixir is a compiled language, so your code is transformed before it executes. (Mix handles compilation for us, and files are only recompiled when they change.) Elixir's compiler reads your files from top to bottom to construct the modules and functions that are used in your application.

This is a big departure from Ruby, where code is evaluated and executed at runtime. Many new Elixir developers get confused by what is compile time and what is runtime. The difference matters because you can introduce subtle bugs—or absolute show-stoppers—without being able to identify where the problem is. This section will equip you with just enough to minimize that confusion.

The simplest explanation is everything inside of a function is executed at runtime, and everything outside of a function is executed during compile time.

Let's demonstrate this with an example. Type the following code at lib/examples/modules/compile.ex:

```
elixir_examples/lib/examples/modules/compile.ex
Line 1  defmodule Examples.Modules.Compile do
   -      IO.puts "I'm at compile-time"
   -
   -      @now Time.utc_now()
   5
   -      def runtime do
   -        IO.puts "This was compiled at #{@now}. It is #{runtime_now()}"
   -      end
   -
  10      defp runtime_now do
   -        Time.utc_now()
   -      end
   -    end
```

The @now statement on line 4 is called a module attribute. Module attributes are set during the compilation phase and hold a value or list of values. They are used like read-only variables inside of your module.

When you run this example, note the compile-time message and the differences in timestamps.

```
$ iex -S mix
Compiling 1 file (.ex)
I'm at compile-time

iex> Examples.Modules.Compile.runtime()
This was compiled at 20:26:17.999151. It is 20:26:19.832422
```

```
iex> Examples.Modules.Compile.runtime()
This was compiled at 20:26:17.999151. It is 20:26:47.052395
```

And if you open iex -S mix again, you won't see the "I'm at compile-time" message. You'll see the message again when you change the module and Elixir recompiles it.

This gets to the heart of the confusion for many new Elixir developers. They will put a value inside of a module attribute (@now in our example) and assume that it updates every time they use it. Instead, this type of code is executed at compile time and the value doesn't change.

A great way to avoid a problem is to put everything in functions when you are starting out. Whether you are accessing the database, collecting a system configuration variable, or reading a file, do it in a named function.

You'll bump up against this more as you write Elixir code. The good news is that the language maintainers have put a lot of work into making it obvious where the compile-time boundaries are. So, issues about compilation have steadily decreased over time.

Wrapping Up

Elixir can be strange to look at when you first start out, but its surface area is fairly small and easy to learn. Putting it together into a meaningful application is where the fun begins.

Elixir comes with a common set of data types and operators. These largely behave as you would expect, but a few rough edges sometimes trip up new Elixir programmers. You'll be set up for success by simply knowing that these edges exist.

Modules and functions are the building blocks of an Elixir application. Modules are containers of functions that you have grouped together. There are a few keywords that make modules more enjoyable to work with. The most powerful is the use keyword, which offers a hook point for library authors to create seamless domain-specific languages.

Functions are conceptually simple, but quite a few syntaxes are available to use in different situations. You'll most commonly use named functions, but you'll work with anonymous functions as well. Plus, Elixir comes with powerful function overloading capabilities.

It's easy to get tripped up when going from an interpreted language to a compiled language. Elixir's compiler transforms your text files into the modules and functions that make up your application. Put all of your code into named functions when starting out. This will prevent compile time versus runtime bugs from tripping you up. The easiest thing to remember when starting is that everything inside of a function is executed at runtime, and everything outside of a function is executed during compile time.

You have seen the basics of Elixir's syntax, but we didn't go into how you use it to create data structures. The next chapter is all about defining and iterating over your application's data structures.

## CHAPTER 3

Working with Data

Conceptually, most software applications can be simplified to this: collect data, operate on data, and then return data to the user. This simplification avoids a whole host of complexities (user interface, database, and so on), but it holds true more often than not. Data and operations on that data are basically the entirety of an application.

In the previous chapter, you learned that functions and modules are used to organize your application. Functions do the work of your application, but they operate on data. So, the way that your data is defined has a big impact on how easy it is to write functions. Luckily, Elixir gives you all of the tools needed to create a clean data layer.

We'll explore two of the data types that we didn't cover in the previous chapter: lists and maps. You'll see the most common ways to create and interact with these data types. You'll also learn how to implement a clean data layer using a special type of map. Finally, we'll go over how you can iterate and modify your data structures.

We'll start with lists.

Lists—Not Arrays

Lists contain data and can be enumerated on. On the surface, they are similar to Ruby arrays, but there are pretty significant differences under the hood that result in totally different performance characteristics. As a result, you'll use lists differently in Elixir than you would in Ruby.

In addition to lists, there's a list alternative that throws a bit of a wrench at new Elixir programmers. You'll learn about tuples and how they differ from lists. Don't worry though, it's a pretty straightforward difference.

The Basics

Lists are represented with the bracket [] syntax. You can easily create them, add to them, and work with them just as in Ruby. Enter the following code in an IEx session:

```
$ iex
iex> list = [1, 2, 3]
[1, 2, 3]

iex> list ++ [4, 5]
[1, 2, 3, 4, 5]

iex> list -- [2, 3]
[1]

iex> [0 | list]
[0, 1, 2, 3]

iex> length(list)
3
```

++ concatenates the second list onto the end of the first. This is equivalent to list + list in Ruby.

-- removes the first occurrence of the right list from the left. This is similar to list - list in Ruby but differs from it because Ruby removes all occurrences and Elixir only removes a single occurrence.

[element | list] adds the given element to the beginning of a list. This is useful for performance reasons, which we'll cover shortly.

The List[1] module provided by Elixir has many utility functions in it. One function that seems to be missing from the module is a function that gets the length of a list. Elixir provides length/1 in the Kernel module, so you can invoke length(list) directly.

Tuples

Tuples appear to be similar to lists but are used completely differently. Tuples are fixed-size containers that are efficiently stored in memory. Enter the following code in an IEx session to see them in action:

```
$ iex
iex> tuple = {:ok, 1}
{:ok, 1}

iex> tuple_size(tuple)
2
```

---

1.   https://hexdocs.pm/elixir/List.html

You *can* manipulate a tuple with functions, but you really shouldn't. The reason is that they are fixed-size containers and operations on them are more costly.

When you add to the beginning of a list, it's a quick operation that touches a minimal amount of memory. When you add to a tuple, it completely recreates the data structure in memory.

Tuples are often used to represent the success or failure of a function or as containers for functions with multiple return values. It's easiest to see this in a real Elixir function:

```
$ iex
iex> File.read("./")
{:error, :eisdir}

iex> File.ls("./")
{:ok, ["your", "files"]}

iex> File.read!("./")
** (File.Error) could not read file ".": illegal operation on a directory
```

Similar to Ruby, the convention is to put a ! symbol at the end of a function if it raises an error. This is why there are File.read!/1 and File.ls!/1 functions that raise errors instead of returning a tuple result.

Tuple results play well with pattern matching, so you can easily handle the success or failure of an operation without catching errors. This is considered pragmatic Elixir and is commonly seen. We'll cover that in the next chapter.

Performance Dangers

Lists look similar to Ruby arrays, so it's easy to think that you can use them the same way. But there's a nonobvious risk that you may run into. Elixir lists are linked lists with O(n) performance on many common operations.

This section needs a disclaimer. You'll likely not run into problems in your everyday usage of Elixir lists due to how large a list would need to be to give you problems. However, it's still an important topic to understand when learning Elixir, or if you're implementing algorithms in Elixir. Elixirists use lists a lot, so they're quite useful despite any performance dangers.

When you access an element in an Elixir list, the entire list up to that element is traversed. As you perform operations on a list that's large, the CPU requirements and time needed to complete the operation increase.

List performance is why it's not common to access list elements by index in Elixir. It's common in Ruby to access a list element using a list[5] syntax or to set a value with list[5] = "five". The Elixir language doesn't provide a convenient syntax to access lists using index positions. Some functions let you access a list by index, but they aren't often used.

One pragmatic example of this is that you'll rarely see if length(list) == 0. The length/1 function is O(n), and there's a better way to make this comparison. Instead, use if list == [] to check if a list is empty. This is quick and doesn't involve iterating over the list. This applies to any data structure—Elixir is very efficient at checking data equality.

Keyword Lists

There's a special type of list that has its own syntax. A keyword list consists of tuple-pair elements in a list where the first element is an atom. This definition is a little complex, so it's best to see it in action by entering this code into IEx:

```
$ iex
iex> [hello: 1]
[hello: 1]

iex> [hello: 1, another: "value"] == [{:hello, 1}, {:another, "value"}]
true
```

Elixir expresses keyword lists with shorthand syntax of [atom: value, atom: value]. They are most commonly used to pass options into a function. For example, create lib/examples/modules/keyword_list.ex and enter the following code:

elixir_examples/lib/examples/modules/keyword_list.ex
```
defmodule Examples.Modules.KeywordList do
  def maybe_print(arg, opts) do
    print? = Keyword.get(opts, :print?, true)

    if print? do
      IO.puts("printing #{arg}")
    end

    arg
  end
end
```

Then run it in IEx:

```
$ iex -S mix
iex> alias Examples.Modules.KeywordList
iex> KeywordList.maybe_print(1, [])
printing 1
1

iex> KeywordList.maybe_print(1, print?: false)
1
```

```
iex> KeywordList.maybe_print(1, print?: false, example: "unused")
1
```

You didn't need to put the keyword list in [] brackets. This is a syntax convenience when a keyword list is the last argument to a function.

Although this syntax seems to be visually similar to keyword arguments in Ruby, the differences between Elixir keyword lists and Ruby keyword arguments are actually quite significant.

The Keyword[2] module has all of the functions you'll need to read or modify keyword lists. You'll commonly use the functions Keyword.get/3, Keyword.put/3, and Keyword.merge/2.

Let's move on to another core data type—maps.

Maps—Your Data Layer Foundation

Maps are the most important data type in your Elixir toolbox. A map consists of key-value pairs, where the key and value can be any data type. In practice, you'll use maps to hold and pass around all of the data in your application.

The Basics

Maps are created with the %{} syntax. You can create an empty map or set the initial key-value pairs in the map. Try it out in IEx:

```
$ iex
iex> empty = %{}
%{}
iex> populated = %{key: "value", another: "entry"}
%{another: "entry", key: "value"}
iex> Map.get(populated, :another)
"entry"
iex> populated[:another]
"entry"
iex> populated.another
"entry"
```

You'll notice that the second map came out in a different order than we typed. Maps aren't in the same order as you added the keys. Smaller maps (of 32 keys or less) are ordered, but you should never rely on the order of a map.

---

2. https://hexdocs.pm/elixir/1.14/Keyword.html

You can put any key or value into a map, but only atom keys can use the key:
value shorthand. If you want to set a key that isn't an atom, then you have to
use the => syntax, like this:

```
iex> map = %{1 => "an integer", 2 => %{another: :map}}

iex> Map.keys(map)
[1, 2]

iex> Map.values(map)
["an integer", %{another: :map}]

iex> Map.get(map, 1)
"an integer"

iex> map[1]
"an integer"

iex> map.1
# SyntaxError
```

Elixir's Map[3] module is used to read and modify maps. This is a commonly
used module, so you should look over it to see what's available to you. There
are lots of functions in the Map module, but here are a few of the basic ones:

```
iex> map = %{}
iex> map = Map.put(map, :key, :value)
%{key: :value}

iex> map2 = Map.put(map, "list", [])
%{key: :value, "list" => []}

iex> map
%{key: :value}

iex> [Map.get(map, :key), Map.get(map, :not_in_map)]
[:value, nil]

iex> Map.delete(map2, "list")
%{key: :value}
```

Maps don't have the same performance problem that lists have. They are
implemented to be very efficient, so you can access or modify maps by key
without concern.

The previous example highlights a core concept in Elixir: data is immutable.
Map.put/3 was used on the map variable, but the original map wasn't changed.

Let's take a closer look at immutability.

---

3.   https://hexdocs.pm/elixir/1.14/Map.html

Immutability

Immutability refers to whether a piece of data can be changed once it's created. The previous section showed how maps are immutable, but this applies to all data types in Elixir.

Immutability also applies across function boundaries. Let's write some code to demonstrate this. Create lib/examples/modules/immutable.ex and enter the following code to see immutability in action:

```
elixir_examples/lib/examples/modules/immutable.ex
defmodule Examples.Modules.Immutable do
  def map_change(map) do
    Map.merge(map, %{a: 1, b: 2})
  end
end
```

```
$ iex -S mix
iex> map = %{number: 1}

iex> Examples.Modules.Immutable.map_change(map)
%{a: 1, b: 2, number: 1}

iex> map
%{number: 1}
```

We passed the map variable into map_change/1, but the original map didn't change.

Immutability makes it significantly easier to reason about data as it's passed around because we know that a variable's data cannot change unless we reassign the variable.

Immutability is a bit of a double-edged sword, though. In Ruby, you can directly modify hashes, lists, or object values. In Elixir, you must iterate and rebuild the data structure to change it.

The best solution to this—and most other things—is practice. As you learn how to effectively use Enum and Map functions, you'll become more comfortable with immutability. We'll dig further into data enumeration later in this chapter.

Structs

You can use maps to store all of your key-value data, but they are missing a few conveniences. Maps aren't named, so you can't tell the purpose of a map without inspecting the contents. Maps don't have the concept of required keys or default values, which means you would have to implement protection in your code. There's a special type of map—structs—that solves these problems.

Structs are maps, but they have additional features added to them. Structs are named maps that have predefined keys, required keys, and default values.

Let's model an SMS message using a struct. Create lib/structs/sms.ex and add the following code:

elixir_examples/lib/examples/structs/sms_1.ex

```elixir
defmodule Examples.Structs.SmsBasic do
  defstruct [:from, :to, :body]
end
```

And then run it:

```
$ iex -S mix
iex> sms = %Examples.Structs.SmsBasic{}
%Examples.Structs.SmsBasic{body: nil, from: nil, to: nil}

iex> is_map(sms)
true

iex> is_struct(sms)
true

iex> sms = %Examples.Structs.SmsBasic{to: "111-222-3333"}
%Examples.Structs.SmsBasic{body: nil, from: nil, to: "111-222-3333"}

iex> sms = Map.put(sms, :body, "A text message")
%Examples.Structs.SmsBasic{
  body: "A text message",
  from: nil,
  to: "111-222-3333"
}

iex> sms = %Examples.Structs.SmsBasic{nope: true}
** (KeyError) key :nope not found
```

You initialized the struct by writing the name of the module between the % and { symbols. By default, all of the provided keys are nil. You can initialize the struct with data, just like a map, but the keys must be part of the defined set or you get an error. Once you have the struct initialized, you use Map functions to manipulate it.

The way that structs are defined means that you can only have a single struct defined in a single module. If you want multiple structs, you need to create multiple modules.

Let's take our struct a step further by implementing required and default-value keys. Rewrite the module to the following code:

```
elixir_examples/lib/examples/structs/sms_2.ex
defmodule Examples.Structs.Sms do
  @enforce_keys [:from, :to]
  defstruct @enforce_keys ++ [:body, status: "delivered"]

  def other_party(sms) do
    case sms.status do
      "delivered" -> sms.to
      "received" -> sms.from
    end
  end
end
```

```
$ iex -S mix
iex> sms = %Examples.Structs.Sms{}
** (ArgumentError) the following keys must also be given when
    building struct Examples.Structs.Sms: [:from, :to]

iex> sms = %Examples.Structs.Sms{to: "you", from: "me"}
%Examples.Structs.Sms{body: nil, from: "me", status: "delivered", to: "you"}

iex> Examples.Structs.Sms.other_party(sms)
"you"
```

There's nothing stopping you from initializing this with bad data, but required keys (via the @enforce_keys module attribute) and default values significantly improve the developer experience of your application data structures.

The function other_party/1 demonstrates a common technique of putting functions that operate on a struct in the same file as the struct. Let's see how this is used to implement contained data structures.

Implementing Data Structures

Data is the heart of programming. You need to be able to create clean data structures so that you can hold, read, and modify data easily. Doing this well will make it easier to read and maintain software applications.

Ruby is object-oriented. So, you write a class that has instance variables and public or private methods. You modify the data through these methods and build your program by implementing your application domain through classes. At runtime, classes are initialized as objects that hold a specific set of data.

But Elixir is functional. It doesn't have classes, and data is immutable, so you might be scratching your head at how to go about implementing your data structures. We can take what we've learned so far—modules, functions, and structs—to implement a clean data layer.

Create a new file at lib/examples/structs/conversation.ex and add the following code:

elixir_examples/lib/examples/structs/conversation.ex

```elixir
defmodule Examples.Structs.Conversation do
  defstruct [:other_party, messages: []]

  def new(sms_list) do
    other_party = List.first(sms_list) |> Examples.Structs.Sms.other_party()
    %__MODULE__{other_party: other_party, messages: sms_list}
  end

  def append(conversation, sms) do
    new_messages = conversation.messages ++ [sms]
    Map.put(conversation, :messages, new_messages)
  end

  def clear(conversation) do
    Map.put(conversation, :messages, [])
  end
end
```

And try it out:

```
$ iex -S mix
iex> alias Examples.Structs.{Conversation, Sms}
iex> from_me = %Sms{from: "me", to: "you", status: "delivered"}
iex> from_you = %Sms{from: "you", to: "me", status: "received"}
iex> convo = Conversation.new([from_me])
%Examples.Structs.Conversation{
  messages: [
    %Examples.Structs.Sms{
      body: nil, from: "me", status: "delivered", to: "you"
    }
  ],
  other_party: "you"
}

iex> convo = Conversation.append(convo, from_you)
%Examples.Structs.Conversation{
  messages: [
    %Examples.Structs.Sms{
      body: nil, from: "me", status: "delivered", to: "you"
    },
    %Examples.Structs.Sms{
      body: nil, from: "you", status: "received", to: "me"
    }
  ],
  other_party: "you"
}
```

This example combines the things you've learned so far in a way that you'll likely see in an Elixir application. The one new concept is the __MODULE__ variable. This is called a compilation environment macro,[4] and it returns the current module name as an atom.

It's common to have a new function in the same module that defines the struct, which takes arguments to build the struct. Another common pattern is modifier functions that take the struct as the first argument and return a modified version.

This technique allows structs and classes to feel similar to each other, even though they are different things. But you'll still need to enumerate over your data structures to read or modify them. Let's look at some techniques for doing that.

Enumerating Data Structures

You'll perform two types of operations on your data. Iteration reads the contents of the data structure, so you can do something meaningful with it. Map (or reduce) transforms the contents of the data structure to modify it or to create something totally different.

Elixir has several options for iterating and mapping your data structures. We're going to look at a few of the built-in options that Elixir gives for iteration and mapping. We'll cover the Enum module and comprehensions.

Enum Module

The Enum[5] module is arguably the most useful module in the standard library. It does lots of things, but we'll cover some of the most commonly used functions. It's built on top of the Enumerable protocol, which lets us enumerate maps and lists out of the box.

Enumerable Protocol

Protocols allow code to change behavior based on the input data. Enum relies on the Enumerable protocol to support all of the functions in the Enum module.

You can implement a protocol for any data type or struct. This means that your own data structure could implement Enumerable and you could use Enum functions with it.

The use case varies for protocols, but it's not a beginner-level feature. So we won't cover protocols in this book.

---

4. https://hexdocs.pm/elixir/Macro.html#expand_once/2
5. https://hexdocs.pm/elixir/1.14/Enum.html

Enum.each

Enum.each/2 is used to iterate over an enumerable. Anything in Elixir that implements the Enumerable Protocol can be enumerated over, but you'll most frequently enumerate lists and maps. Enum.each/2 doesn't return any value from the iteration. Because Elixir is immutable, you cannot modify data that exists outside of the enumeration function.

Let's enumerate a map using Enum.each/2:

```
$ iex
iex> Enum.each(%{a: "value", b: "another"}, fn {key, value} ->
      IO.puts "Key: #{key}; Value: #{value}"
    end)
Key: a; Value: value
Key: b; Value: another
```

Maps are key-value pairs, so the enumeration function accepts each value in a tuple pair. This is an example of how tuples are frequently used for fixed-size data types.

One of the techniques that's common in Ruby apps is to define an empty hash, iterate over some data, build up the hash as you go, and then return the hash. You can't do that in Elixir because data is immutable. The next example demonstrates what happens if you try to. This Elixir code compiles and runs, but the final result is empty:

```
iex> result = %{}

iex> Enum.each([1, 2, 3], fn i ->
  result = Map.put(result, i, true)
end)

iex> result
%{}
```

You'll see a warning that "variable result is unused" when you run this example, and the final result is unchanged. If you want to build up a result, you'll need to use different functions, like Enum.map or Enum.reduce.

Enum.map

Enum.map/2 is one way to transform data. It returns a new list based on the result of the function you give it:

```
$ iex
iex> Enum.map([1, 2, 3], & &1 * 2)
[2, 4, 6]

iex> Enum.map([%{a: 1}, %{a: 2}], & Map.put(&1, :a, "updated"))
[%{a: "updated"}, %{a: "updated"}]
```

Each item in the list is passed into the provided function, and the return value of each function is returned inside of a new list. The number of elements in the list does not change: if five elements are in the input list, five elements are returned.

Enum.reduce

Finally, Enum.reduce/3 iterates over each value in a list and transforms the accumulator. The accumulator can be any value that you want. Here's an example of a reduce function that finds the largest value in a list:

```
$ iex
iex> Enum.reduce([1, 2, 3, 1], 0, fn num, accumulator ->
  if num > accumulator do
    num
  else
    accumulator
  end
end)
3
```

The return value of each iteration becomes the next iteration's accumulator. You can build up any result that you want with this technique. You could build a new map, modify a custom struct, or keep track of a single value or multiple values.

Here's the same code in Ruby:

```
$ irb
irb(main)> [1, 2, 3, 1].reduce(0) do |accumulator, num|
  num > accumulator ? num : accumulator
end
```

Functionally, these are similar. But the actual syntax between Ruby and Elixir is quite different.

reduce takes a bit of time to get used to. But once you do, it becomes an important tool for iterating over data structures.

Comprehensions

Comprehensions[6] are a built-in syntax for iterating and reducing data. Comprehensions use the for keyword, but it's nothing like a traditional for-loop. Comprehensions can iterate a single source of data, combine multiple sources of data, filter data, and reduce data into any result format.

---

6.   https://hexdocs.pm/elixir/Kernel.SpecialForms.html#for/1

Try out these comprehensions in an IEx session:

```
$ iex
iex> for i <- [1, 2, 3], do: i * 2
[2, 4, 6]

iex> for i <- 1..6,
        Integer.mod(i, 2) == 0,
        into: %{},
        do: {i, "even!"}
%{2 => "even!", 4 => "even!", 6 => "even!"}
```

The first example is the most basic form of a comprehension and is likely what you'll use most of the time. The second shows features that turn comprehensions into a powerful tool.

The Integer.mod(i, 2) == 0 clause acts as a filter for the data. Elixir checks the data against this function and only executes the iteration function if the result is truthy. In this case, it's checking if the remainder of i / 2 is 0, which is true only for even numbers.

The into: option puts the result into the given data structure. In our example, a map is returned instead of a list. By default, comprehensions are returned as a list (equivalent to into: []), so you only need to type this out if you want the result in something other than a list.

The next example extracts data from the Conversation struct that we created earlier. This is presented as a .exs file, but type it out in an IEx shell.

```
$ iex -S mix
```

elixir_examples/convo.exs
```
alias Examples.Structs.{Conversation, Sms}

from_steve = %Sms{
  from: "Steve", to: "Reader", status: "delivered"
}

from_reader = %Sms{
  from: "Reader", to: "Steve", status: "received", body: "text"
}

other = %Sms{
  from: "+1-222-333-4444", to: "Steve", status: "received"
}

failed_other = Map.put(other, :status, "failed")

convos = [
  Conversation.new([from_steve, from_reader, from_steve]),
  Conversation.new([other, failed_other]),
]
```

```
for convo <- convos,
    message <- convo.messages,
    String.starts_with?(message.from, "+1") or message.from == "Reader",
    message.status == "received" do
  {message.from, message.body, length(convo.messages)}
end
# => [{"Reader", "text", 3}, {"+1-222-333-4444", nil, 2}]
```

This example iterates over each convo, iterates over each message, filters to only include messages that start with "+1" or "Reader", filters to only include received messages, and then constructs a result based on the message and conversation. That's a lot of stuff in a small amount of code!

This code would be more verbose if we wrote it using Enum functions, so comprehensions provide a clean syntax for data enumeration. But it's totally okay to use Enum. Start with the technique you feel most comfortable with.

Wrapping Up

A clean data layer makes it easier to work with, maintain, and extend a software application. Elixir provides a whole host of data types, but lists and maps are among the most important as you model an application's data.

Lists hold any data in your application. They are easy to work with, but their performance characteristics mean that you need to be a bit cautious about how you use them. Keyword lists are a special type of list that are most commonly used to pass around options in your application.

Maps are the heart of an application's data layer. They are simply containers that hold key-value pairs, but their performance and ease of use make them the most common data type. Structs are a special type of map with additional features like specified fields, required fields, and default values. At their core, structs are just maps, so they are easy to work with.

You can create self-contained data structures by putting the functions that modify or read your data structures into the same module that defines the struct. Elixir provides several options for how you can iterate or reduce a data structure. The Enum module and for comprehensions are usually the best options for working with a complex data structure.

Up next, we're going to cover one of the most exciting features in the Elixir language—pattern matching.

## CHAPTER 4

Pattern Matching Your Way to Success

Pattern matching will change the way that you write code. It's a simple—yet extremely powerful—feature that's built into the foundation of Elixir. Pattern matching is used in function definitions, variable assignments, and control flows—it's a core port of the language's design. And once you master it, you won't want to go back.

In Ruby (and most languages), the core structures for control flow are if statements. This is easy to use if you want to check whether a value is one of two candidate values—true or false. It becomes cumbersome if you want to check whether a value is one of many possible values—based on string contents, array values, map keys, and so on. Elixir has if statements, but it also has something more powerful.

In this chapter, you'll see how Elixir's case statement completely replaces if and switch statements. Elixirists use case statements a lot, so it's good to get comfortable with it. Luckily, it's also simple. You just need to know how pattern matching works. The syntax of pattern matching is simple, but its roots run deep and it takes a little bit of practice to get used to. This chapter builds up slowly so that you have everything you need to be confident with patterns.

We'll start by looking at the most basic forms of pattern matching. Then, you'll see how case statements are used in control flow. Finally, we'll combine everything to see how pattern matching affects function definitions and makes recursive functions much easier to write.

Pattern matching is a game changer, so let's dive in!

Pattern Matching Basics

Elixir doesn't have a normal assignment operator. In most languages, the = operator is used for simple left = "value" statements. In Elixir, this operator is called the match operator, and it initiates pattern matching.

Pattern matching is implemented by the BEAM, so it's baked into the runtime of the language. Some optimizations make it efficient even for a large number of pattern clauses. So, you can use pattern matching without worrying about a negative performance impact on your application.

In this section, we'll go over different pattern-matching syntaxes for basic data types, lists, maps, tuples, and more.

Match Basic Types

Let's start with the most basic syntax for pattern matching. Open a new IEx session and type the following:

```
$ iex
iex> 1 = 1
1

iex> a_number = 1
1

iex> 1 = a_number
1
```

This first example is seemingly simple, but 1 = 1 is rather unusual. In Ruby, you can only have variables on the left side of =. Clearly, that's not the case here.

To evaluate a pattern mentally, execute the right side and then compare the result with the left side. Assign any variables that are on the left side. If the patterns don't match, then you get a MatchError:

```
iex> 1 = 2
** (MatchError) no match of right hand side value: 2
```

Variable assignment works just as it does in Ruby. Values are reassigned when they're on the left side:

```
iex> a_number = 1
iex> a_number = 2
iex> a_number
2
```

It's important to understand that this doesn't transform the data of the variable. It simply reassigns the variable to a different value.

One thing that trips up many new Elixir programmers is that you cannot have function calls inside of the pattern.

```
iex> 1 + 1 = 2
CompileError: cannot invoke remote function :erlang.+/2 inside a match

iex>
defmodule Local do
  def call do
    test() = 1
  end

  defp test do
    1
  end
end
```

```
** (CompileError): cannot find or invoke local test/0 inside match.
   Only macros can be invoked in a match and they must be defined
   before their invocation. Called as: test()
```

This is a useful error message. It tells us about our coding error and also lets us know that some functions (macros) can be invoked in a match clause.

It's not common to write macro-based match functions yourself, but you'll frequently use ones provided by Elixir. Besides lists and maps—which we will cover next—string concatenation is commonly used. Here's an example that uses string concatenation (<>) in a match clause:

```
iex> "store:" <> data_command = "store:Widget:process"
"store:Widget:process"

iex> data_command
"Widget:process"
```

The <> appears on the left side of the = symbol, and a variable is used where a string part would be. Elixir pattern-matches the string and extracts the relevant text into the data_command variable.

This is a powerful way to split apart text without calling String.split/2. But it's not without its limitations. The variable must always be the last part of the concatenation. You can do this:

```
iex> "text" <> ":" <> number = "text:7"
iex> number
"7"
```

But you can't do this:

```
iex> "text" <> symbol <> number = "text:7"
** (ArgumentError) the left argument of <> operator inside a match
   should always be a literal binary because its size can't be
   verified. Got: symbol
```

Even with this limitation, it's still extremely useful.

Let's explore other powerful pattern-matching forms. We'll look at lists, maps, and tuples next.

Match Data Structures

Lists, tuples, and maps are fully compatible with pattern matching. You'll commonly use this in two ways. The first is to extract data structure components into variables so you can operate on them. The second is to check if an input matches a certain structure, as part of control flow.

This section focuses on extracting the components of data structures. Open a new IEx session and type the following:

```
$ iex
iex> [a] = [1]
iex> a
1

iex> {:ok, result} = {:ok, "my result"}
iex> result
"my result"

iex> [a, 2, c] = [1, 2, 3]
iex> {a, c}
{1, 3}

iex> [a] = [1, 2]
** (MatchError) no match of right hand side value: [1, 2]
```

Lists and tuples can be matched on an exact-position basis. Each position on the right and left must have compatible patterns. You can even separate a data structure into multiple variables, like a and c in the previous code. If your structure doesn't match the pattern provided, you get a MatchError.

Parts of a list are matched with the | and ++ operators:

```
iex> [head | tail] = [1, 2, 3, 4]
iex> head
1

iex> tail
[2, 3, 4]
```

```
iex> [first, second | rest] = [1, 2, 3, 4]
iex> {first, second}
{1, 2}

iex> [first, second] ++ rest = [1, 2, 3, 4]
iex> {first, second}
{1, 2}
```

The | operator is used inside of the list brackets to represent the beginning of the list. One or more elements can be matched at a time.

The ++ operator is used to capture the concatenation of two lists. It's less common to see this syntax, though.

One thing you'll notice from these match clauses is that they behave exactly like their function versions. This makes the syntax intuitive to use. If you can use <> or [|] in your code, then you can use it in a pattern match clause. For example:

```
iex> [1, 2] ++ [3, 4]
[1, 2, 3, 4]

iex> [1, 2] ++ rest = [1, 2, 3]
iex> rest
[3]
```

In this example, we're able to use the ++ operator as a function (left ++ right) and as a match.

Pattern matching with maps is also intuitive, as in the following example:

```
iex> %{a: a} = %{a: 1, b: 2}
iex> a
1

iex> %{a: 1, b: nil} = %{a: 1, b: 2}
** (MatchError) no match of right hand side value: %{a: 1, b: 2}

iex> %{list: [%{a: ["a"]}, %{b: [b]}]} = %{list: [%{a: ["a"]}, %{b: ["b"]}]}
iex> b
"b"
```

This example is a bit dense, but it shows you that the complexity of the match clause isn't limited as long as it uses valid syntax.

Map matching behaves differently than lists because maps don't have to perfectly match. In the first example, the left side doesn't mention the b key at all. Maps are loosely matched when the key isn't specified. This is useful in practice because you often extract a few keys of a map. Here's a simple example to demonstrate this:

```
iex> [] = [1]
** (MatchError) no match of right hand side value: [1]
iex> %{} = %{a: 1}
%{a: 1}
```

The left side of the list match is empty, and it doesn't match the right side list. The left side of the map match is empty, but it still matches the right side map. Maps are loosely matched, but lists are strictly matched.

Let's see how we can reference existing values in a pattern match clause.

Pinned Values

You are not limited to only assigning variables in a pattern match. The pin operator lets you use the value of an existing variable inside of your pattern match. This is most useful in test suites, where you want to guarantee that different values match inside of a data structure.

Prepend the variable with the ^ symbol to pin its value. Let's see this in action:

```
iex> var = :match
iex> ^var = :match
:match

iex> ^var = :no_match
** (MatchError) no match of right hand side value: :no_match

iex> [^var, second] = [:match, :other]
iex> second
:other
```

Pinned values are strictly enforced, so the result must perfectly match or you'll receive an error. This is intuitive for most data types, but be careful with maps:

```
iex> map = %{a: 1}
iex> ^map = %{a: 1}
%{a: 1}

iex> ^map = %{a: 1, b: 2}
** (MatchError) no match of right hand side value: %{a: 1, b: 2}
```

The map didn't exactly equal the pinned value, so a MatchError was thrown.

You might be wondering what happens if you use a variable twice on the left side of a match. This isn't considered a pinned value, but it behaves similarly.

```
iex> {x, x} = {1, 1}
iex> x
1

iex> {x, x} = {1, 2}
** (MatchError) no match of right hand side value: {1, 2}
```

The duplicated variable must be equal in all positions of the match clause. Otherwise, you'll get a MatchError.

Now that you have the basics of pattern matching, let's see how it can be used to control the flow of a program.

Use Patterns for Control Flow

Pattern matching goes well beyond assigning variables. Control flow—the branching logic of your application—is performed with pattern matching. Most programming languages rely on if statements for all (or close to all) of an application's control flow. But Elixir offers more choices.

We'll go over four control flow structures: if, case, with, and cond. They all have different purposes and situations where you'll use them, but case statements are the most commonly used.

Let's start with if statements.

If Statements

If statements are so common that it would be a bit strange for Elixir to not have them. Elixir's if statements work largely like you're used to. Use if to quickly check whether a value is truthy or falsy. Here's an example of a simple if statement:

```
$ iex
iex>
if 3 > 5 do
  "if body"
else
  "else body"
end

"else body"
```

Sometimes you'll see if statements on a single line. Elixir allows this single-line syntax for many different keywords:

```
$ iex
iex> if 6 > 5, do: "if body", else: "else body"
"if body"
```

If statements are used to check a single value for truthiness. They can't be used to split a value apart or to compare multiple potential values at the same time. Often, Elixirists will reach for other control flow structures instead of if statements due to these drawbacks. But that doesn't mean if statements are bad! You'll still frequently see and use if statements.

How Elixir Implements If Statements

 Elixir implements if statements as a macro that expands to a single case statement. You can see this in the Elixir Kernel source.[1]

This means that if statements are a subset of case statements. A case statement can do everything that an if statement in Elixir can do, but it can do additional things as well.

Elixir doesn't provide an else if syntax. You can nest if statements to create this type of comparison waterfall, but it quickly becomes messy. Instead, case and cond statements are well-suited for checking multiple potential match values. Let's look at case statements now.

Case Statements

A case statement evaluates a given term (any piece of data) against multiple potential patterns. The first pattern that matches the term executes a given block of code.

Case statements are the most commonly used and foundational control flow structure. Use case to check a single term against a number of potential patterns. The first clause that matches will have its body executed and returned.

The next code example demonstrates a case statement with multiple clauses:

```
$ iex
iex>
case {:ok, "a string"} do
  :not_a_match ->
    IO.puts "will not run"

  {:ok, string} ->
    IO.puts(string)
    "return value"
end

a string
"return value"
```

This case statement evaluates each pattern against the given term {:ok, "a string"}. The first term doesn't match, so its code is ignored. The second term does match, so the code is executed and its value is returned.

Case statements are meant to be exhaustive. This means that every possible outcome should be checked against, or else you'll receive a CaseClauseError:

---

1. https://github.com/elixir-lang/elixir/blob/v1.14.1/lib/elixir/lib/kernel.ex#L3720

```
$ iex
iex>
case "fail" do
  false -> nil
end
```

`** (CaseClauseError) no case clause matching: "fail"`

If you want to include a fallback in your case statement, capture the result into a variable:

```
$ iex
iex>
case "passed" do
  false -> nil
  var -> "It #{var}!"
end
```

`"It passed!"`

Use _ instead of a variable name if you want to match any value but you don't use the value in your code. This special variable name tells Elixir that you are intentionally not using the variable, so the compiler won't emit a warning.

Remember, you can have any number of case clauses in a case statement. It's a best practice to keep the number of clauses to a manageable size (up to three), but you have the ability to use as many as needed.

Case statements are used to match a single term against many patterns. There's a different control flow structure that adds pattern matching to a series of operations. Let's take a look at with statements next.

With Statements

A common task in programming is to run many functions and expect a successful result at each step. The final result of all of the functions together is what you want, but an error at any step results in the whole operation failing.

Elixir's with statements capture the successful outcome of a series of operations, plus there's a built-in way to handle any errors. Use with statements when you have several operations—especially if they are prone to failing—that must all succeed to return a result.

Here's an example of hypothetical code—that doesn't use a with statement—showing a chain of function calls:

```
{:ok, response} = MyApi.request()
{:ok, json} = Jason.decode(response)
{:ok, status} = Map.fetch!(json, "status")
```

This isn't necessarily bad, but handling errors becomes cumbersome. We would check each line against possible error responses and handle an error appropriately. With statements make this easier for us to implement.

A with statement consists of clause lines, followed by a main body, followed optionally by else clauses. Each clause line (pattern <- term) is evaluated top to bottom until all are evaluated, or until one of the lines doesn't match. Once all lines are matched, the main body is executed and its value is returned.

If a line doesn't match and there's an else body, then the else is evaluated like a case statement is. It pattern-matches against the error value based on your provided error handling code. You use this opportunity to gracefully handle the error—log it out, throw an exception, return an error tuple, and so on. If there isn't an else body, then the result that didn't match is directly returned.

Here's an example of multiple steps coming together to produce a result. Any of these steps could fail, and we want to gracefully handle the result:

```
$ iex
iex>
with {:ok, files} <- File.ls("."),
     [first_file | _rest] <- Enum.sort(files),
     {:ok, %{ctime: created}} <- File.lstat(first_file) do
  IO.puts("The file #{first_file} was created at #{inspect created}")
else
  {:error, _} -> {:error, "file system failed"}
  [] -> {:error, "no files"}
end

# Your result will vary
The file .DS_Store was created at {{2022, 9, 21}, {20, 43, 29}}
```

One thing that trips up new Elixirists is using = instead of <- in a with statement. This will compile and even run, but any failure that would normally have triggered the else clause will instead raise a MatchError. If you accidentally do this, you may be unpleasantly surprised because the with statement loses its error-handling ability.

What happens if we run this code in a directory that doesn't have any files in it? Create a new empty directory and start iex in it:

```
$ mkdir empty && cd empty
$ iex
iex> # same code from previous example
{:error, "no files"}
```

In this case, the Enum.sort(files) line returns an empty list [], so the pattern [first_file | _rest] doesn't match. The else statement is evaluated and [] matches this pattern, so the error clause executes and an error tuple is returned.

With statements are useful if your function has many steps that could fail, such as issuing, parsing, and handling an external HTTP request. If you want to gracefully handle any errors, use with.

Let's look at the last control flow structure, cond.

Cond Statements

The last control flow structure at our disposal is the most simple. A cond statement evaluates a number of clauses until the first truthy value is reached. The first matching clause will execute the body statement. Elixir doesn't provide an else if syntax, but cond statements fill this gap.

The other control flow structures are more commonly seen than cond is, but it still has its place. Use a cond statement when checking multiple separate expressions at once. And when your check uses a function (like String.contains?/2), then you have to use a cond statement because you can't use functions inside of pattern matches. Let's take a look:

```
$ iex
iex>
cond do
  false -> "no"

  true ->
    IO.puts "Multiple-lines can be used"
    "yes"
end

# Output:
Multiple-lines can be used
"yes"
```

The power of cond is that you can execute functions in the clauses—something that you cannot do with pattern matching. So you can check any statement:

```
$ iex
iex> str = "The fox jumped over the dog"
iex>
cond do
  String.contains?(str, "z") -> "not this"
  2 * 2 == 100 -> "certainly not this"
  length(String.split(str, " ")) >= 5 -> "5 words or more"
end

"5 words or more"
```

If none of the clauses evaluate truthy, you'll receive a CondClauseError. Add true -> as the final clause for a fallback that guarantees a match.

Let's switch gears to see how pattern matching affects functions.

Level Up Your Functions

Pattern matching takes function overloading to a new level. The most basic type of function overloading lets you define the same function name with a different number of arguments, but Elixir supports more than this.

We'll go over function overloading, how it's implemented, and how it can be used to create seamless recursive functions. But first, we need to cover a helpful addition to pattern matching called guards.

Guards

While pattern matching is really powerful, it can't do certain things. Pattern matching operates on the structure of a value, but sometimes we want to go beyond that. For example, we may want to know whether a number is within a certain range, whether a value is in a predefined list, or what the type of a value is. Guards let us do all of these things.

Guards are statements that use functions or operators to add additional checks to a pattern match. They can be used anywhere that pattern matching is used: case and with statements, comprehensions, and function definitions. Plus, you can write your own guards—as long as they follow limitations enforced by Elixir's compiler. But that's not common, so we won't cover it in this book.

Let's start with a simple example. We'll use a guard to check whether an integer is within a particular range. The guards appear after when in each line:

```
$ iex
iex> number = 7
case number do
  n when n < 5 -> :low
  n when n >= 5 and n < 10 -> :medium
  n when is_number(n) -> :high
end

:medium
```

Try this example out with different values for number. Use 0, 10, and "string". Let's consider what happens if you put "string" into this case statement. We get a CaseClauseError, despite it matching n in every single clause. The guards that appear after when cause the value to match nothing.

Certain guards start with is_, such as is_number, is_bitstring, is_map, is_list, and so on. These are used as a form of type checking. They only are checked at runtime, so it's not going to offer compile errors to you, but it's incredibly useful to guarantee that your functions will only operate on certain types of data.

The functions that can be used with guards are limited. This is for your own good though—guards are guaranteed to not mutate data and their performance can be optimized. The Elixir documentation[2] has a great breakdown of available guards, limitations, and how to write your own guards.

Let's look at function overloading next.

Overloading with Pattern Matching

A function in Elixir can be defined with multiple function heads—each function head is a definition of that function for a specific pattern. When a function is called, the first function that matches the provided arguments is used. So, you can define my_func/2 multiple times with different patterns.

Let's write a to_bool/1 function that works with multiple function heads. In your examples project from the previous chapter, create lib/examples/patterns/boolean.ex:

elixir_examples/lib/examples/patterns/boolean.ex
```
Line 1  defmodule Examples.Patterns.Boolean do
   -      @false_s ["", "undefined", "false", "nil", "null", "-0", "0", "no", "off"]

          def to_bool(bool) when is_boolean(bool), do: bool
   5
   -      def to_bool(0), do: false

   -      def to_bool(nil), do: false

  10      def to_bool(str) when is_bitstring(str) and str in @false_s, do: false

   -      def to_bool(str) when is_bitstring(str) do
   -        String.downcase(str) not in @false_s
   -      end
  15
   -      def to_bool(_), do: true
   -    end
```

Run test values through it to see it working:

```
$ iex -S mix
iex> import Examples.Patterns.Boolean

iex> to_bool(0) # false
iex> to_bool("0") # false
```

---

2. https://hexdocs.pm/elixir/guards.html

```
iex> to_bool("undefined") # false
iex> to_bool("UNDEFINED") # false
iex> to_bool(false) # false

iex> to_bool(true) # true
iex> to_bool("A string") # true
iex> to_bool(1) # true
```

Even though we've defined to_bool/1 over five times, everything still works as expected. A mix of pattern matching and guards pulls this off for us.

An example of guard limitations is seen on line 10. We would ideally check the input value in a case-insensitive way, but there's no way to do this in the guard. A solution to this is seen on line 12. The input is guarded as a string, and then the function body performs the downcasing.

The final trick is seen on line 16. This function accepts any value, so to_bool/1 is guaranteed to always have a matching function. If you remove this line, you'll see a FunctionClauseError for inputs like to_bool(1).

The Secret to Function Overloading

There's no magic in Elixir's function overloading—it's entirely based on things you already know! And once you know how it works, you'll better understand why functions are evaluated from top to bottom.

A function with multiple heads gets converted to a single function consisting of a case statement. A more basic to_bool/1 function might look like this:

elixir_examples/lib/examples/patterns/boolean_case.ex
```elixir
defmodule Examples.Patterns.BooleanCase do
  def to_bool(value) do
    case value do
      bool when is_boolean(bool) -> bool
      0 -> false
      nil -> false
      str when str in ["undefined", "false"] -> false
      _ -> true
    end
  end
end
```

This is all handled by the Elixir compiler, and it completely explains the top-to-bottom definition order. If we define a function that accepts any value at the top of our file, then it will be first in the case statement and will always be triggered. This also shows that guards work in case statements because they're converted to case statements by Elixir's compiler.

Recursion with Pattern Matching

Recursion is the most primitive form of iteration and reduction in Elixir. A recursive function is one that calls itself. If a function can call itself, it needs some idea of when to stop. This is called the base case, and every recursive function needs one, or it will execute infinitely.

Some problems are most easy to solve when thought about recursively. Because of this, you'll often see recursion appear in libraries or even in your own code. It's a little scary at first, but you'll appreciate its value as you get comfortable with it.

Pattern matching goes hand in hand with recursion because you can build the base case using pattern matching. The most practical example of this is list iteration. Create lib/examples/patterns/recursion.ex with the following code:

elixir_examples/lib/examples/patterns/recursion.ex

```
Line 1  defmodule Examples.Patterns.Recursion do
          def biggest_number(list) do
            biggest_number(list, nil)
          end
     5
          defp biggest_number([], max), do: max

          defp biggest_number([head | tail], current_max) do
            next_max = max(head, current_max || head)
    10      biggest_number(tail, next_max)
          end
        end
```

```
$ iex -S mix
iex> Examples.Patterns.Recursion.biggest_number([2, 1, 5, 1])
5

iex> Examples.Patterns.Recursion.biggest_number([])
nil
```

Line 2 is a public function definition that accepts a single argument. This allows biggest_number/1 to be called without worrying about the accumulator (current_max) being set.

Line 6 is the base case for when the input list is empty. This function relies on pattern matching to execute only when the list is empty. It returns the accumulated biggest_number, which gets returned back to the function caller.

Line 8 is the main body of the recursive function. The argument list uses pattern matching to grab the first element of the input list (head) and the rest of the input list (tail). The function then calculates the maximum value and recursively invokes itself.

When you write a recursive function, you're always moving forward in the input. In this case, our list elements are iterated one by one, and the reduced value at the end is the biggest value in the list.

One great thing about Elixir is that you don't need to worry about having a recursive function that runs too long. Elixir is tail-call optimized, which means that it doesn't create a new stack entry for the final function call inside of a function. So you won't ever see a StackOverflow exception. Of course, you still need your base case or your function will run forever.

Wrapping Up

Pattern matching is one of the standout features of Elixir. You'll frequently use pattern matching, so it's important to get comfortable with it. The most basic form of pattern matching is the match operator =. Use the match operator to break values apart or for simple variable assignment. Pattern matching works with any term in Elixir, so you can use it for lists, maps, or any other data type.

Pattern matching is crucial in most of Elixir's control flow structures. case is the most common and foundational control flow structure. Use it to check a term against a number of candidate patterns. Use with to capture the successful outcome of a series of operations or to handle an error if something goes wrong. Finally, use cond when you need to check a statement's truthiness without the limitations of pattern matching.

Functions seem straightforward, but pattern matching supercharges them. You can overload a function not only with the number of arguments but also with pattern matching. Define the same function multiple times with different patterns in order to build recursive functions or functions that have different behavior for different input arguments.

Along with pattern matching, parallelism is often touted as Elixir's strength. The next chapter is all about processes, parallelism, and GenServers.

## CHAPTER 5

GenServers: Build Cities, Not Skyscrapers

Elixir has one of the best concurrency models of any programming language today. In fact, there's a good chance that you're reading this book because you heard big claims about Elixir's ability to scale automatically across all CPU cores. The hype is real, and you're going to understand how it works by the end of this chapter.

Parallelism and concurrency have always been hot topics, but they are especially important when we're designing high-performance systems that run at low cost. A system with a high degree of parallelism is able to handle more simultaneous requests—from a web browser, an async job system, and so on—on fewer machines.

Ruby and Elixir have different concurrency models. In fact, Elixir has a concurrency model that's unlike pretty much any other mainstream language. We'll be going over those differences in this chapter, in addition to defining foundational terms that are important for you to understand.

We'll look at exactly how BEAM processes work and what makes BEAM processes so special. You'll spawn basic processes and then evolve them into GenServer processes. You'll learn that GenServers are actually not magic but are simply a well-built abstraction on top of the BEAM's process model. Finally, we'll bring it all together by thinking about how the BEAM's process model lets us build entirely different types of systems than we would build in Ruby or other languages.

But first, there's a little disclaimer that's necessary before you dive into the chapter.

You Don't Need GenServer

This chapter is very important, but it's going to teach you something that you won't use immediately. However, you'll be better prepared to debug your application, run your application in production, and test your application when you understand the material in this chapter.

The reason why you won't use this material immediately is because good Elixir libraries (certainly the ones presented later in this book) use best practices to ensure that they are stable and give you the best possible starting point. Phoenix, Ecto, and Oban will ensure that your application is scalable and error-resilient.

These libraries are designed to not only be appropriately parallel but to also handle errors. They use OTP best practices to help prevent your application from getting in a bad state. You don't know these best practices yet, so your system will be better if you use the libraries.

You'll eventually need GenServers, and you definitely should understand how the process model works from day one. But you may not need to write code that uses them for some time. Instead, lean on the libraries that Elixir experts have written to achieve what you need. At some point, you'll need to write your own GenServer, and you'll be ready to do so.

Let's start this chapter by comparing parallelism and concurrency.

Parallelism vs. Concurrency

It takes a bit of time to fully grasp parallel computing. It's okay if you don't pick it up all at once. But, to give you the best shot, let's start at the ground floor. We'll look at what concurrency and parallelism are and then go into how Ruby and Elixir operate in these areas.

Concurrency Is Not Parallelism

The terms parallelism and concurrency are the source of a lot of confusion. While they seem interchangeable, they refer to distinctly different, but related, topics.

Concurrency is the ability to *coordinate* multiple tasks at the same time. Imagine that there's a single CPU core on a server. Concurrency allows that single CPU core to weave together and execute tasks that are necessary to serve requests. From an outsider's perspective, it would appear that requests are handled at the same time.

But that's not necessarily true. Concurrent tasks are coordinated in such a way that they overlap in their execution, but their execution may or may not be done at the same point in time. We need parallelism to execute different tasks at the same point in time.

Parallelism is the ability to *execute* multiple tasks at the same time. Imagine that there are multiple CPU cores on a server. Parallelism allows those CPU cores to work at the same time to execute different tasks simultaneously. Multiple CPU cores are required for this to work because a single CPU core can only run one set of instructions at a time.

Parallelism provides advantages when it comes to system throughput and overall performance. A parallel system will be able to fully use its compute resources to serve requests. You often require less CPU to serve the same requests when adding parallelism to an application.

Concurrency is a property of programming languages, but the actual implementation of that language determines how parallelism is achieved. It's possible to have a concurrent language that isn't parallel, for example. In fact, you'll learn about this next.

Let's go into how Ruby's concurrency works.

Ruby's Concurrency Model

Ruby uses threads to achieve concurrency. In Ruby, Thread.new runs a block of code concurrently with other code in that process. Concurrent code can finish in any order. Here's a simple example that uses Thread.new to print out characters. If you run this code multiple times, you'll see that the print order changes.

```
irb> Thread.new{ puts "a" }; Thread.new{ puts "b" }
a
b
irb> Thread.new{ puts "a" }; Thread.new{ puts "b" }
b
a
```

Ruby threads share memory. This means that you can change a variable in one thread, and reading that variable in another thread will reflect the changed value. This isn't a bad thing by itself, but it leads to a whole class of programming bugs called race conditions.

To solve these race conditions, you often need to reach for Thread::Mutex[1] to coordinate memory access between different threads.

Shared memory is especially risky in multi-tenant SaaS environments where a bug could lead to data being accessed by the wrong users in an application.

Concurrency in Ruby becomes very complex as a system scales, so many Ruby developers don't use threads. Instead, it's more common to run everything top-to-bottom in a single thread. Relatively new changes are happening in Ruby that add a new option for true parallelism. We'll look at that new parallelism option later in this section.

Parallelism in Ruby

Different Ruby implementations are available today. The most common, by far, is MRI Ruby. This section will focus on that implementation due to its popularity.

MRI Ruby doesn't have parallelism within a single process. There's a Global Virtual Machine Lock (GVL) that prevents multiple threads from executing in a process at the same time. This is because the Ruby Virtual Machine isn't internally thread-safe, so you really don't want multiple things running in parallel.

The way around this in Ruby has traditionally been to fork multiple Ruby processes. Popular libraries like Puma and Sidekiq take this approach to parallelism (in addition to multi-threading for increased concurrency). Each forked process has its own GVL, so they run fully in parallel with each other. But memory requirements become multiplicative for each process, so machines need to have more RAM to do this in practice.

MRI Ruby is the most popular Ruby implementation. There are other implementations like JRuby and TruffleRuby that are implemented on top of virtual machines that provide parallel execution. There can be compatibility issues and other tradeoffs with these implementations though, which is why their popularity hasn't increased.

Ruby Ractors

Ruby Ractor[2] is a new actor-model abstraction that provides thread-safe concurrency and parallel execution in Ruby. This is very exciting! It's fairly new, so we haven't seen how it will change Ruby, but it has a lot of promise.

---

1. https://docs.ruby-lang.org/en/3.2/Thread/Mutex.html
2. https://ruby-doc.org/core-3.0.0/Ractor.html

Ractors don't share memory, so they can only access memory that they own. Ractors communicate with each other by sending messages, which are then received and handled.

This is actually similar to how Elixir's concurrency model works. Let's explore that next.

Elixir's Concurrency Model

Elixir uses processes to achieve concurrency. Don't be fooled by the name because Elixir's processes are not operating system processes. Instead, these processes are lightweight virtual processes implemented by the BEAM. The BEAM's process implementation forms the foundation for all code execution.

Processes don't share memory with each other—they can only access their own memory. (We'll cover some exceptions to this later in this chapter.) Processes send and receive messages between themselves to coordinate work. Messages are stored in a process mailbox. This lines up closely with how Ractors in Ruby work, which makes sense because both the BEAM and Ractors are actor-based.

Actors are the foundation of concurrency in actor-based programming. Each actor receives messages (from other actors) and then processes each message. Actors can respond to messages, send messages to other actors, or execute code locally. This lines up exactly with how Elixir works.

In Elixir, a process executes work by taking a message out of its mailbox—it will always process messages in the order that it receives them. The message is then executed by the process, and this process repeats. Processes can execute infinitely—always waiting for a new message—or they can be set to only handle a fixed number of messages.

A process can only ever execute one message at a time. This means that there's no concurrency inside of a process. This is an often overlooked benefit of Elixir's concurrency model. In Elixir, you're in complete control over whether code runs in parallel or not.

Parallelism in Elixir

If there's no concurrency within a process, you may be wondering how the BEAM executes code in parallel. The magic comes from the ability to have tens of thousands of processes (or more!) executing concurrently with each other.

The BEAM uses schedulers to coordinate and execute functions on a CPU. By default, one scheduler is available for every logical CPU processor. So a quad-core hyper-threaded CPU will have eight schedulers. Each scheduler has a run queue that holds information about which processes are requesting execution.

Schedulers execute functions until either the process is done or a certain amount of work (called reductions) has occurred. If this happens, that process is kicked off of the scheduler and placed at the back of a run queue. This means that an infinite loop in Elixir will run forever, but it will only hold up a CPU for a fixed number of reductions at a time. This property is great for building scalable systems because a high-CPU request won't dramatically affect other requests on that server.

This explains how Elixir scales across your CPU without any work from you. By correctly using processes, you automatically get CPU scalability. And all of the major libraries use processes in the right way, so following the best practices in this book will set you up for success!

Let's take this knowledge and put it into action by implementing several different processes in Elixir.

Explore Elixir Processes

Processes are the foundation of concurrency in Elixir. They are small, easy to spawn, and you can run as many of them as you have memory for—in production, tens to hundreds of thousands would be normal. You don't need to know much about the BEAM's process architecture to use processes, but the details highlight how powerful they are.

In addition to being scalable, processes form the foundation of durable Elixir applications. Processes are able to crash without taking down the rest of the system. This durability is one of the main traits of the BEAM.

We're going to cover the basics of processes in this section, but we'll also cover some of the interesting details of the process architecture. You'll learn how to spawn a process and pass messages to it, and you'll make an infinitely running process that responds to incoming messages. We'll also go over error isolation, memory isolation, and garbage collection.

Spawn a Process

Elixir makes it easy to start a new process. The spawn/1 function takes a function and executes it inside of a new process. Let's do that in IEx:

```
iex> self()
#PID<0.109.0>

iex> pid = spawn(fn -> IO.puts("Hello from #{inspect self()}") end)
Hello from #PID<0.112.0>
#PID<0.112.0>

iex> Process.alive?(pid)
false
```

We pass a function into spawn/1 that prints out some information about the executing process. Your exact numbers will be different than mine, but notice that the spawned function prints out as 0.112.0 and the originating process is 0.109.0. This is called a process ID (PID) and is one of the core data types in Elixir. The difference in PIDs proves that the spawned function is actually executing inside of a different process.

This spawned process would be useful if we wanted to fire off some asynchronous code, but it's not really that useful right now. We need to be able to send messages into the process and receive responses from it in order to turn it into a useful tool. The receive function lets us do just that. And, to send a message to the process, we'll use the send function.

Type this code into your IEx session:

```
iex> pid = spawn(fn ->
  receive do
    :hello -> IO.puts("Hello World")
    {:hello, name} -> IO.puts("Hello #{name}")
  end
end)
iex> Process.alive?(pid)
true

iex> send(pid, :hello)
Hello World
:hello

iex> Process.alive?(pid)
false
```

We were able to process the message :hello and see that the correct output was printed. If you try the example again with send(pid, {:hello, "Your Name"}), you'll see that it responds with a different message. The receive function uses pattern matching to determine which code to run, just like you're already familiar with from Chapter 4, Pattern Matching Your Way to Success, on page 49.

We aren't going to do the exercise here, but if you wanted to receive a response from the spawned server, you would use send to respond back to the originating process. This requires you to pass the PID of the current process as part of the message and then to receive a response. That's pretty cumbersome, but by the end of this chapter, you'll see how GenServer makes this easy.

Our process is no longer alive after a single message—it terminated after its code finished executing. Let's make it process messages forever.

Process Messages Forever

Recursion is very useful to create infinite loops. Usually, an infinite loop would be a bad thing, but it's totally fine when used in a controlled way.

Create lib/examples/spawn/infinite.ex and add the following code:

elixir_examples/lib/examples/spawn/infinite.ex
```elixir
defmodule Examples.Spawn.Infinite do
  def start do
    spawn(& loop/0)
  end

  defp loop do
    receive do
      {:add, a, b} ->
        IO.puts(a + b)
        loop()

      :memory ->
        {:memory, bytes} = Process.info(self(), :memory)
        IO.puts("I am using #{bytes} bytes")
        loop()

      :crash ->
        raise "I crashed"

      :bye ->
        IO.puts("Goodbye")
    end
  end
end
```

The start/0 function uses spawn/1 to kick off our looped process. The loop function is simple—it's just a receive block with a variety of messages handled. For all messages, except :bye, the loop/0 function is called as the last thing the function does. This creates a recursive loop that will handle messages forever. Let's try it out:

```
$ iex -S mix
iex> pid = Examples.Spawn.Infinite.start()

iex> send(pid, :memory)
I am using 2608 bytes
```

```
iex> send(pid, {:add, 1, 2})
3
iex> send(pid, {:add, 50, 50})
100
```

You could extend this exercise by turning loop/0 into loop/1 and keeping track of state for each message. If you did this, you would have a server that changes state based on messages it has received from the outside world. This is a pretty small change but is still pretty cumbersome. Don't worry, GenServer will make this easy for us too.

Before we get into GenServer, let's look at some of the interesting details of how processes are implemented. These may seem unimportant at first, but they drastically shape the runtime characteristics of an Elixir application.

Error Isolation in Processes

There's an argument to be made that the genius of the BEAM is not its parallel execution ability but, rather, its ability to isolate errors. Let's put that into perspective: if two requests come into a web server at the same time, and one of the requests crashes, then we wouldn't expect the other request to also crash.

Let's spawn two processes and then crash one of them to create a basic demonstration:

```
$ iex -S mix
iex> p1 = Examples.Spawn.Infinite.start()
#PID<0.161.0>

iex> p2 = Examples.Spawn.Infinite.start()
#PID<0.163.0>

iex> send(p1, :crash)
[error] Process #PID<0.161.0> raised an exception
** (RuntimeError) I crashed

iex> [Process.alive?(p1), Process.alive?(p2)]
[false, true]
```

This is a simple example, but it serves to demonstrate that we didn't have to do anything to isolate this error. In fact, it wouldn't be possible to crash one of these processes from the other. Of course, an event like a database failure is going to cause errors all over an application, but that would be due to an external factor rather than an internal one.

It's easy to take error isolation for granted. Frameworks in languages that don't provide error isolation use clever programming to make it feel like there's isolation, but a guarantee from the virtual machine runtime is another level of confidence.

Process Memory Architecture

Each process in Elixir has its own memory space. This consists of a heap and a stack that grow toward each other. Eventually, if they are unable to grow, the BEAM will allocate more memory to the process.

Processes start off with a fairly small amount of memory. On my computer, I see 2608 bytes taken up for a brand new process:

```
$ iex -S mix
iex> pid = Examples.Spawn.Infinite.start()
iex> Process.info(pid, :memory)
{:memory, 2608}
```

Process.info(pid) is a useful source of information about any process that's actively running. It tells you things like heap size, stack size, reductions (which roughly equate to CPU usage), and the number of unprocessed messages. Here, we used Process.info/2 to return a focused version of the available data.

Data in Elixir is copied between processes. So, if you send a message to a process, that memory will be duplicated and then passed as a message. This has benefits for small bits of data, but it would be a bit of a waste to copy every single message between processes. Elixir has a little trick up its sleeve to optimize copies.

Elixir uses a binary heap[3] to globally store large (> 64 bytes) binary data. This binary heap is shared between processes and uses reference counting to determine when the memory can be cleaned up. Because the BEAM uses immutable data, you don't need to worry about this causing bugs in your application. The memory here is safe to use and can be referenced by multiple processes without fear.

The small memory size of processes is part of what makes them easy to spawn and destroy. But sometimes you'll find yourself debugging a problem where too much memory is being used. So, let's cover how garbage collection works.

Garbage Collection

Garbage collection isn't fun, right? Actually, the BEAM's garbage collector is rather interesting. I wrote about this in fairly deep detail in *Real-Time Phoenix* [Bus20], so we'll cover much less in this book.

---

3. https://www.erlang.org/doc/apps/erts/garbagecollection#binary-heap

Because each process in Elixir has its own memory heap and stack, each process performs its own garbage collection. The binary heap that was mentioned in the previous section is globally shared, so there's a global collection process to handle it. However, it's relatively lightweight because the binary heap uses reference-counted binaries.

Each garbage collection process runs fast because it deals with less memory, and it happens on a cycle according to how much that process is churning data. If the process is frequently processing messages or is running out of memory, it will experience a collection cycle more often than a process that isn't doing much.

But you have to be cautious of a hidden danger. Sometimes long-lived processes can take up more memory than they need, but they won't undergo a garbage collection cycle because they aren't active enough to kick one off. In this situation, a process can take up more memory than it needs for a long period of time. Let's create an artificial example:

```
$ iex -S mix
iex> pid = Examples.Spawn.Infinite.start()
iex> Enum.each(1..1000, & send(pid, {:add, &1, &1}))

iex> send(pid, :memory)
I am using 62816 bytes
```

Your numbers may vary here, but you should expect to see that this number is higher than the 2.6 KB that it started out as. This doesn't immediately make sense because our process has no state, and it has processed all of its messages. So, why is it taking up thirty times more memory?

The issue here is that the process mailbox lives on the heap of the process. As we inundated it with messages, it had to allocate more memory to hold those messages. The garbage collection process only occurs based on running out of memory or processing a given number of reductions—neither of which is occurring.

We can manually trigger garbage collection with :erlang.garbage_collect(pid). Once you do this and query the process memory, you'll see that it's back to its starting size.

```
iex> :erlang.garbage_collect(pid)
iex> send(pid, :memory)
I am using 2608 bytes
```

The number of long-lived processes is usually small enough that this doesn't matter. But, if it becomes a problem, then look at the ERL_FULLSWEEP_AFTER system variable and set it to a number like 20. This causes garbage collection to run more frequently—at the cost of a bit more CPU. This flag is enabled on every single production system I've worked on, and it has never caused problems for me—mainly because frequent garbage collection is fast and handled on a per-process basis.

There's another option to prevent memory bloat. You can put individual processes into a hibernation state. A hibernating process has its memory reduced as much as possible. But when the process receives a message, it will incur a cost to exit the hibernation state and handle the message. GenServer[4] has a hibernate_after option that will automatically enter hibernation when the GenServer is idle.

Both techniques are important to know about, but you likely won't need to use them for some time. Frameworks like Phoenix use hibernation with sane defaults so that you often don't need to think about it.

Now that you have the basics of processes down, let's take a look at how Elixir makes them easy with GenServer.

Go Parallel with GenServers

Processes are the lowest-level concurrency primitives in Elixir, but it's pretty rare to use them directly. Instead, you'll use libraries that let you build processes without worrying about the details. GenServer stands for "generic server," and it's the most common process library.

GenServer is part of OTP, so it's actually written in Erlang. Elixir provides the GenServer module to seamlessly bring this Erlang library into Elixir. It's a very important library, so it has been integrated into the language very well.

GenServer solves a few problems that you have already seen:

State Management
    A GenServer stores state and makes it available to all message handlers. This state can be modified in response to a message.

Seamless Messaging APIs
    GenServer provides functions to synchronously call into the process or to asynchronously cast into the process. These functions are built using send and receive. Plus, they handle cumbersome details like timeout, responses, and so on.

---

4.   https://hexdocs.pm/elixir/GenServer.html

Prebuilt Best Practices

When you use processes directly, small problems pop up that can lead to errors. For example, you could send a process an incorrect message that it doesn't receive. If you did this, the process mailbox would slowly fill up and exhaust your system memory. GenServer builds in best practices to ensure things like this don't happen.

Now, it's time to create a GenServer. It's actually easier than creating a process!

Write Your First GenServer

We're going to focus on four different functions in this example: init, handle_cast, handle_call, and handle_info. These are special function names that GenServer uses to call your code properly.

Create lib/examples/gen_server/simple_server.ex and add the following code:

```
elixir_examples/lib/examples/gen_server/simple_server.ex
Line 1  defmodule Examples.GenServer.SimpleServer do
   -      use GenServer
   -      require Logger
   -
   5      def start_link(init_args, name: name) do
   -        GenServer.start_link(__MODULE__, init_args, name: name)
   -      end
   -
   -      def init(speaker: speaker) do
  10        {:ok, %{speaker: speaker, last_result: nil}}
   -      end
   -
   -      def handle_cast(
   -        :announce,
  15        state = %{speaker: speaker, last_result: result}
   -      ) do
   -        Logger.info("#{speaker}: The last result I computed was #{result}")
   -        {:noreply, state}
   -      end
  20
   -      def handle_call({:add, a, b}, _from, state) do
   -        result = a + b
   -        {:reply, result, %{state | last_result: result}}
   -      end
  25  end
```

Spin up an IEx instance to test this out:

```
$ iex -S mix
iex> alias Examples.GenServer.SimpleServer
iex> {:ok, pid} = SimpleServer.start_link([speaker: "Genny"], name: nil)
{:ok, #PID<0.149.0>}
```

```
iex> GenServer.call(pid, {:add, 5, 10})
15

iex> GenServer.cast(pid, :announce)
:ok
[info]  Genny: The last result I computed was 15
```

Let's break each function down to understand what is happening. The start_link/2 function on line 5 starts the GenServer and kicks off initialization. start_link is able to pass initialization arguments into the process. We're using this to accept a speaker parameter that's placed in the GenServer state.

The init/1 function on line 9 receives the provided arguments and starts with a given state. Maps or structs are great for state because they are easy to update and access in the message handlers.

GenServer.cast/2 sends a message to the process. The handle_cast/2 callback on line 13 is then invoked with the message contents and the state of the process. Cast messages are asynchronous, which means that the calling process doesn't receive a reply and won't wait for the message to be processed.

GenServer.call/2 sends a message to the process. The handle_call/3 callback on line 21 is invoked with the message contents, some info about the calling process, and the state of the process. Call messages are synchronous and will wait for a default 5 seconds before raising an error. Call messages receive a response, which allows you to extract information from the GenServer.

The init, handle_cast, and handle_call functions are all executed inside of the GenServer process. start_link, GenServer.cast, and GenServer.call are all performed inside of the calling process.

Expand Our GenServer

It's rare to use GenServer functions directly outside of a GenServer-implemented module. It's a best practice to create wrapper functions that invoke them for you. Put these helper functions above start_link/2:

```
def announce(server \\ __MODULE__) do
  GenServer.cast(server, :announce)
end

def add(a, b, server \\ __MODULE__) do
  GenServer.call(server, {:add, a, b})
end
```

This code does the exact same thing as calling the GenServer functions manually, but callers no longer need to concern themselves with the internals of GenServer.

There's one final GenServer callback that's important to know about. Modify the existing init/1 function:

```
def init(speaker: speaker) do
  :timer.send_interval(5000, :announce)
  {:ok, %{speaker: speaker, last_result: nil}}
end
```

And add a corresponding handle_info/2 at the bottom of the file:

```
def handle_info(
  :announce,
  state = %{speaker: speaker, last_result: result}
) do
  Logger.info("#{speaker}: The last result I computed was #{result}")
  {:noreply, state}
end
```

handle_info/2 looks similar to handle_cast/2, but it's used for non-GenServer messages. For example, if you send a message to this process, then it's handled by the handle_info/2 callback. We use the :timer.interval/2 function to automatically send a message to the process every five seconds.

When you start this process, you'll see a message every five seconds:

```
$ iex -S mix
iex> alias Examples.GenServer.SimpleServer
iex> {:ok, pid} = SimpleServer.start_link([speaker: "Genny"], name: nil)
{:ok, #PID<0.149.0>}

iex> SimpleServer.add(5, 10, pid)
15
[info] Genny: The last result I computed was 15

iex(5)> SimpleServer.add(50, 70, pid)
120
[info] Genny: The last result I computed was 120
[info] Genny: The last result I computed was 120
...continues forever
```

The GenServer process will log out its last result forever because the process runs until it's explicitly exited. We won't get into the details of all of the ways that a process can exit, but you do have full control of how a process terminates.

Is a GenServer an Object?

A common reaction when seeing GenServer is to think "oh, that's an object!" Objects and GenServers have a lot in common. They both hold state, the modifications to the state are colocated in code, they receive messages (at least in Ruby), and they can respond to the messages they receive. But GenServers are not objects, and you should not treat them like objects.

It's important to consider that GenServers are a concurrency mechanism and objects are a programming development primitive. Their runtime performance characteristics are also completely different. You can create and destroy many more objects per second in Ruby than you could processes in Elixir—simply because Ruby objects are lighter weight and are designed to be created and destroyed rapidly.

Another aspect that GenServers handle that objects don't is time. Every program that we write runs over a period of time. Often, we want to do things based on a certain frequency. An object in Ruby lacks the ability to easily deal with time. We would need to build that ourselves and deal with all of the challenges that would be introduced. However, we can easily create a GenServer that changes over time by sending messages in an interval.

This time aspect lets you think of GenServers as a living thing. They can change over time (in the constraints that are coded for them). They emit messages to other GenServers in the system. They can be entirely contained or very sociable. They can exist for the duration of a web request, a WebSocket connection, or even exist as long as the system is up. Thinking of them in this way lets you build things that would be considered complex but are intuitive to develop and reason about.

Now that you know how to create a GenServer, let's step back and understand some risks that come with them.

What About Supervisors?

Supervisors are an important type of process in BEAM applications. A Supervisor keeps track of child processes and can strategically restart them if one dies. You'll see a type of Supervisor later in this book when we discuss the Application module.

This book doesn't cover Supervisors because you don't need to know much about them this early in your Elixir journey. As you learn Elixir and get more comfortable, you'll likely end up using them. When that happens, read the Supervisor documentation.[5]

---

5.   https://hexdocs.pm/elixir/1.12/Supervisor.html

Be Parallel, Be Cautious

With great power comes great responsibility. Elixir is a powerhouse when it comes to running parallel processes. You can literally spin up thousands of concurrent requests that are active at the same time. But this can cause problems.

Programs don't exist in a vacuum. They interact with other programs like databases or external APIs. A program can only handle so many parallel requests before it becomes overwhelmed. You could easily exhaust a database connection pool or downstream API service by sending too many simultaneous requests.

It's best to always have control over the amount of parallelism in your system. Libraries that you'll see later in this book, like Ecto and Oban, all include a limited number of parallel processes so that you're less likely to overwhelm your system. You can raise the limits if you have a system that can handle it, or you can decrease them to deal with a resource-constrained system.

Built-in libraries like Task[6] and functions like spawn/1 will let you create one-time processes for parallel execution. This often ends badly if done in an uncontrolled way because it's easy to accidentally create too many simultaneous processes. Instead, stick to plain GenServers or build a data pipeline with a library like Oban to maintain control of your application's parallelism.

I wrote about creating a stable data pipeline in the "Avoid Performance Pitfalls" chapter of *Real-Time Phoenix [Bus20]*, but if you use Oban then you'll be in a good place.

We're going to switch gears to a more conceptual topic. You've learned about processes and established foundations to use them, but this leaves a big question remaining. What does the BEAM's process model allow us to do that we can't do in other programming languages? Let's tackle this next.

Build Cities, Not Skyscrapers

The traditional model of building applications—especially web applications—is single-stack-oriented. This means that applications work from an entry point (web request, CLI command, background worker, and so on) and execute code in a single stack or process to achieve their purpose. This programming model is clearly the dominant one in the Ruby community.

---

6. https://hexdocs.pm/elixir/main/Task.html

This traditional model has its benefits, but it's an uphill battle to work against the grain. It's difficult to colocate web and background workers for cost optimizations. And it's near impossible to create in-memory data structures that are shared across the entire application. Effectively, you end up writing applications a certain way, even if it's not how you want to build the application.

The properties of BEAM processes allow for a completely different style of application development. The entry points to the application are the same, but we are no longer limited to a single stack. In fact, we can build applications that consist of many smaller subsystems that have an API used by other parts of our application. Each subsystem has its own stack, garbage collection, and error handling. But they're all deployed as part of the larger application, so complexity is kept to a minimum.

Think of the traditional stack-oriented programming model as a skyscraper. There's a set of doors at the bottom, and you can go all the way to the top before going back out through the doors. But the BEAM programming model lets us build cities instead of skyscrapers. We have the option of building small purpose-driven subsystems that exist for a single purpose, or we can build large monolithic subsystems that operate just like a stack-oriented system does.

In an Elixir app, you'll have many small subsystems that you don't even think about. Talking to the database is a subsystem. Responding to web requests is a subsystem. Background jobs are a subsystem. They all live under the same application and deployment, but they have their own data and performance constraints. These subsystems communicate with each other via message-passing, so they're connected where it matters.

With Elixir, you can truly build a city of subsystems that all work together to create a cohesive application. You can optimize certain parts of the city that become performance bottlenecks. You can add new subsystems without interfering with the rest. It's a beautiful thing when everything comes together in this way, and the BEAM's process model is what makes it possible.

Wrapping Up

Concurrency and parallelism are tough topics at first, but they can be distilled down to a difference between coordinating multiple tasks and executing multiple tasks at the same time. Ruby is a concurrent language, but the Global Virtual Machine Lock prevents it from executing in parallel. The BEAM is a highly parallel runtime that allows Elixir to seamlessly scale across all CPU cores. This gives it an advantage when it comes to squeezing more performance out of a system for less total cost.

Processes are the foundation of concurrency in Elixir. Processes send and receive messages with other processes, and it's common to run hundreds of thousands of processes in a production system. This is because processes are lightweight, with each having a separate memory allocation and garbage collector.

Processes are easy to work with, but building production systems requires a lot of cumbersome tasks to get right. The GenServer module takes care of these tasks for us. GenServer lets us create long-lived processes that maintain state and process messages easily. There's no magic here though—GenServer is built on top of processes, so we get all of the benefits of processes like error isolation and memory independence.

Elixir is highly parallel, but systems usually can't run at full firepower. It's important to control the amount of parallelism in an application so that you don't overwhelm external systems like databases or APIs. Libraries usually handle this pretty well for you, so you have a good starting place to make sure your application is stable from day one. In fact, existing libraries do so much for you that you may not actually need to worry about GenServers and processes for some time.

The BEAM's process model allows us to build completely different styles of applications than we would otherwise. Instead of traditional single-stack-oriented applications where everything is in one big stack, we can separate our system into smaller subsystems that communicate using message passing. Think of your system as a city that you can expand or shrink easily over time.

This wraps up the first part of this book. The next part of this book is going to see us through a real-world project. You'll learn about the most popular libraries and how they enable you to build scalable applications built on the BEAM's process model.

Part II

Tools of the Trade

You have seen the foundations, but now it's time to build a real application. You'll learn the most popular Elixir libraries that help you solve common problems. You'll interact with a database, build a web interface, write asynchronous jobs, and make outbound HTTP requests. Plus, you'll have a pretty cool application at the end!

## CHAPTER 6

Persisting Data with Ecto

Welcome to Part II! We're going to change things up a bit in the second part of this book. The first part was focused on learning the language and getting comfortable with Elixir, but the second part is focused on learning tools and building a real application. Throughout these next chapters, you'll build an SMS app that sends real text messages. We'll implement new features in each chapter until there's a complete product.

It's important to build things from scratch. That's how you learn the fine details. So, you'll start with mix phx.new and write all of the code yourself. However, some things like CSS styles and HTML are provided in a way that you can easily copy into your application. This is because they are often long code listings that are tedious to type by hand. And don't worry—you can start with a provided code package at the beginning of each chapter if that's your preference.

Data is the foundation of all applications. We ingest data from users or APIs, we manipulate data with queries and processing, and we show users their data so they can act on it. Data persistence and access is a pretty big deal!

Ecto is Elixir's answer for everything data and database-related. Ecto differs significantly from ActiveRecord, but it still feels familiar due to a design that's focused on developer productivity.

We'll start the chapter by going over the project we're going to build. Then we'll cover Ecto's design and the philosophy it takes. Of course, we'll compare it to ActiveRecord along the way. You'll write an Ecto schema to represent SMS messages and then use Ecto changesets to persist data into the database. Finally, you'll learn several different ways to query data and how to best expose data functions to your application. We'll wrap all of our functions into a context that will be used later in the project.

There are entire books (such as the excellent *Programming Ecto [WM19]*) written about Ecto, so there's no way we can cover everything in a single chapter. Instead, this chapter gives you the basics and points you to the Ecto documentation[1] to learn more.

Let's look at the project that we'll be writing during Part II.

What Will We Build?

I love building web applications that interact with the real world in some way. One of the "secret tricks" that has served me well over my career is the use of SMS and Phone to connect applications to users. So, our project is an SMS client that sends and receives SMS using a mock SMS API.

This project is compatible with a real SMS provider—Twilio—and is capable of sending and receiving real SMS messages. However, regulation was passed that requires verification to deliver SMS messages in the USA. Instead, we'll use a mock SMS API that's 100% compatible with Twilio—you could take the project at the end of the book and connect it to a real Twilio account!

Here's what the final product will look like. We'll have a list of SMS conversations on the left and a detailed view of the current conversation on the right:

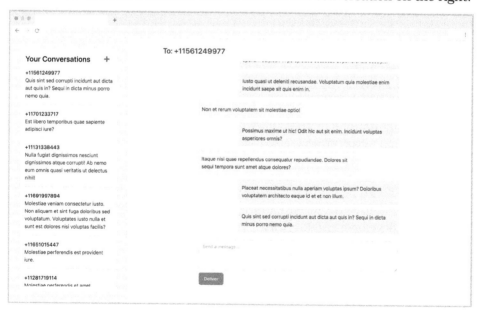

The mock API server is included with this book. It uses LiveView to provide a real-time interface to view the SMS messages that have passed through it. And it uses a GenServer to hold the SMS state. This makes it a great resource to look at after you've completed the project.

To start, we'll generate our application skeleton.

Create an Empty Phoenix App

Phoenix is the primary web development framework in the Elixir ecosystem. It's a bit like Ruby on Rails, although future chapters will talk about how different they are. We aren't going to dig into Phoenix beyond this short introduction yet, but we are going to use its generator to make our initial project directory.

Phoenix's generator provides us with a web server, a database client, and more. Everything is correctly set up from the beginning so it works right out of the box. This gives us the fastest path to using Ecto.

The installation instructions[2] on Phoenix's documentation give us everything we need to get started. Follow along with these directions to get started. Make sure that you have at least Elixir 1.14 and Erlang/OTP 25 installed. (This book uses more recent versions that you can find in Install Elixir on Your Computer, on page 10.)

```
$ mix local.hex
Are you sure you want to... [Yn] Y

$ mix archive.install hex phx_new
Are you sure you want to... [Yn] Y

# It's very important to use the name "phone_app"
$ mix phx.new phone_app
Fetch and install dependencies? [Yn] Y

$ cd phone_app

$ mix ecto.create
The database for PhoneApp.Repo has been created

$ mix test
.....
Finished in 0.2 seconds (0.1s async, 0.1s sync)
5 tests, 0 failures
```

If everything is green with your tests, then you're good to go with the rest of this chapter. If you run into issues, then make sure that you have Postgres installed and that you have the latest versions of Elixir and Erlang.

---

2. https://hexdocs.pm/phoenix/installation.html

Before we jump into Ecto, let's cover the different layers that we're going to build in the upcoming chapters.

Our Application's Layers

We're going to build a complete application over the next chapters. This application consists of several well-structured layers that work together to create the final product. An application can be structured in many different ways, but starting from this perspective is usually a safe bet. As your application develops over time, you may add or remove layers based on your needs.

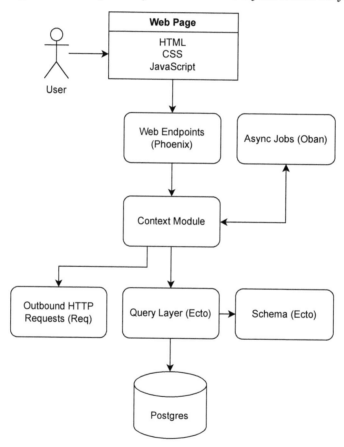

We won't go into each layer at this time, but our application consists of a web UI frontend, Phoenix web endpoints, asynchronous jobs with Oban, outbound HTTP requests with Req, and a data layer powered by Ecto. This chapter is all about the data layer consisting of queries, schemas, and changesets.

Let's jump right in and go over the basics of Ecto!

The Foundations of Ecto

Ecto[3] is an Elixir library for data mapping and database queries. Ecto is language-integrated, so queries are written in a way that feels like Elixir and not a third-party syntax. There are other data access libraries in Elixir, but Ecto is by far the most popular. There are Ecto bindings for PostgresQL, MySQL, MSSQL, and SQLite3, but we'll only use PostgresQL in this book.

ActiveRecord is the most popular data access library in Ruby. ActiveRecord and Ecto have different philosophies, so let's compare them. After that, we'll take a high-level pass over Ecto's concepts.

Ecto vs. ActiveRecord

Both ActiveRecord and Ecto have a significant focus on usability, security, and flexibility. They both feel familiar and powerful after using them for only a small amount of time. But they are implemented with entirely different design patterns. These design differences make them feel like opposites.

ActiveRecord is implemented using the Active Record[4] design pattern. (As a note, this name existed before the ActiveRecord library did.) This design pattern combines data access and persistence directly on the object that holds the data. Everything you do in ActiveRecord happens on the model class directly. Queries, preloads, updates, inserts, and the like all originate from your model classes. If we wanted to fetch and update a Person record, it would look like this:

```
irb> steve = MyApp.Person.find_by(name: "Steve")
irb> steve.update!(name: "Stephen")
```

Ecto is implemented using the Repository[5] design pattern. This pattern requires that all data mapping and query operations happen through a centralized Repository. This creates a different programming experience. Let's take a look at the previous example, implemented using Ecto:

```
iex> steve = Repo.get_by(MyApp.Person, name: "Steve")
iex> changes = Ecto.Changeset.change(steve, name: "Stephen")
iex> Repo.update!(changes)
```

"Magic" is a term that's often used when talking about data access libraries. There will always be some magic when translating between a database and an application—the more removed from the database the app is, the more

---

3. https://github.com/elixir-ecto/ecto
4. https://www.martinfowler.com/eaaCatalog/activeRecord.html
5. https://martinfowler.com/eaaCatalog/repository.html

magical it feels. Magic makes the development experience easier, but it can be much more difficult to reason about in a scaled application. For example, hooks and automatic relationship loading significantly increase debugging time, but they also decrease initial development effort.

Ecto makes a point of reducing magic. Operations are explicit and can be easily reasoned about when reading an application's source code. This philosophy has resulted in Ecto not having hooks or automatic relationship loading, in addition to other small changes that are present throughout the library. Many people love that Ecto gets rid of magic.

In general, Ecto feels more like SQL, but it still protects you when it comes to security and performance best practices. ActiveRecord feels more like accessing an object. This is great in some situations, like querying a system via the Rails console, but it results in more magic that can be difficult to reason about.

Ecto Concepts

There are three main roles that Ecto satisfies: querying the database, translating data from the database into application structures, and providing ways to change data. Here's how Ecto tackles each of these roles:

Query the Database
> Ecto has a built-in query language called Ecto.Query[6] that you use to write queries in Elixir. These queries are securely translated into SQL, and the database executes the query. Ecto makes heavy use of macros, so queries are validated at compile time for security and correctness.
>
> Ecto's Query language isn't SQL, but it feels very similar. It's rare that you are unable to write a query that you want to write. Ecto.Query also lets you load and reference relationships using built-in functions.

Translate Data from the Database
> Ecto schemas[7] map data from your database into an application struct using type definitions provided in a schema. Schemas also define associations between other schemas, and Ecto provides functions to work with these associations.
>
> Schemas don't provide any access to the database, so you don't have to worry about accidental database queries once a schema is realized from

---

6.   https://hexdocs.pm/ecto/Ecto.Query.html
7.   https://hexdocs.pm/ecto/Ecto.Schema.html

the database. For example, you are guaranteed that my_schema.some_field won't result in a database query.

Change and Validate Data

Ecto changesets[8] cast and validate data from external sources into your database. Ecto provides a variety of default validation functions that let you check for the presence of data, ensure data consists of specific values, and more. Plus, you can always add application-specific custom validation.

We'll be diving deeper into each of these concepts throughout the rest of this chapter. Next, let's use Ecto to define our application's data structures!

Write an Ecto Schema

Databases revolve around data, so we need a way to define the types, tables, and relationships of our application's data layer. Ecto solves this with schemas. We use schemas to define our data structure, and then Ecto uses the schema definition to operate on our application's data.

We'll write a schema to hold SMS messages, and then we'll look at how Ecto fields and associations work. Let's jump in!

Phoenix Generators

Phoenix provides a generator that's used to define a schema file and migration file all at once. The reason why we don't use that in this book is simple: I don't like using most generators. I prefer the control of writing the code myself, and it gives me time to think about the schema I'm defining.

Many people like using generators because they allow you to quickly implement commonly repeated code templates. If you want to use the mix phx.gen.schema generator for your own projects, you can read its documentation.[9]

Define an SMS Message Schema

Ecto.Schema uses macros to create a domain-specific language (DSL) that we use to define our schema. This results in a data definition that's easy to read and write. Create a file at lib/phone_app/conversations/schema/sms_message.ex in the

---

8.   https://hexdocs.pm/ecto/Ecto.Changeset.html
9.   https://hexdocs.pm/phoenix/Mix.Tasks.Phx.Gen.Schema.html

phone_app directory that you created earlier in this chapter. Add the following content to it (the field comments are for your reference and don't need to be typed out in your file):

```
phone_app/lib/phone_app/conversations/schema/sms_message.ex
defmodule PhoneApp.Conversations.Schema.SmsMessage do
  use Ecto.Schema

  @timestamps_opts [type: :utc_datetime_usec]
  schema "sms_messages" do
    # 1-to-many relationship with the other person in the conversation
    belongs_to :contact, PhoneApp.Conversations.Schema.Contact

    # Holds the message identifier for Twilio's message objects.
    field :message_sid, :string
    # Holds the account identifier that interacted with Twilio.
    field :account_sid, :string

    # Holds the full text contents of the SMS message.
    field :body, :string
    # The phone number that sent the SMS message.
    field :from, :string
    # The phone number that received the SMS message.
    field :to, :string

    # Holds the current state of the SMS message from Twilio.
    field :status, :string
    # Whether this message was received inbound or sent outbound.
    field :direction, Ecto.Enum, values: [:incoming, :outgoing]

    timestamps()
  end
end
```

Our module starts with a use statement on line 2 that brings the Ecto schema macros into our module. Without this line, the schema/2 function would be undefined and our code wouldn't compile. The schema/2 function on line 5 says that our database table is called sms_messages and its data definition is defined inside of the do block.

Inside of the do block, we use the field macro function to define the individual fields of our data structure. A comment describing each field is included, so you can see how the field fits into our data structure. We'll come back to the belongs_to function later in this section.

We use timestamps/0 to define inserted_at and updated_at fields that Ecto manages for us. When you add a record to the database, Ecto will automatically set inserted_at for you. And when you update the record, the updated_at column will be set.

The @timestamp_opts module attribute on line 4 tells Ecto that our timestamps should include microseconds (usec). Without this, our timestamps would only contain seconds. It can be helpful to have this higher fidelity timestamp when debugging a system, so I recommend that you always use utc_datetime_usec timestamps.

Use the Schema as a Struct

Ecto schemas are just structs, so we can use them with the %Struct{} syntax that you used earlier in this book. Let's try this out with the SMS Message schema. Start an IEx session with the -S mix option and try it out.

(You'll see a warning that the Contact schema doesn't exist, but this is safe to ignore for now. The warning comes from our association referencing a module that doesn't exist. If it becomes a problem and your project won't run, then create the Schema.Contact module found at the end of this section.)

```
$ iex -S mix
iex> alias PhoneApp.Conversations.Schema.SmsMessage
iex> message = %SmsMessage{to: "+1-111-222-3333"}
%PhoneApp.Conversations.Schema.SmsMessage{
  __meta__: #Ecto.Schema.Metadata<:built, "sms_messages">,
  id: nil,
  contact_id: nil,
  contact: #Ecto.Association.NotLoaded<association :contact is not loaded>,
  ...
  to: "+1-111-222-3333",
  ...
}

iex> message.to
"+1-111-222-3333"
```

Because schemas are mapped to structs, you can use most of the same functions and operations that you are used to on structs. (Ecto doesn't implement the Access protocol for schemas, so some features are not available.) For example, you can build a struct using the %{} syntax, and you can modify fields using the Map.put/3 function.

We'll come back to the contact association in a moment, but let's talk about fields first.

Schema Fields

The field/3 macro function has many different options that you can use to define a schema the way you want. We'll cover a few of the different options, but the most important is the field type.

Ecto's "Types and Casting" documentation[10] lists out all of the different field types supported. Field types are either primitives or custom types. These are some examples of primitive fields: :integer, :string, :utc_datetime_usec, :map, and more. You can even specify array fields using the {:array, inner_type} field type.

Ecto.Enum and Ecto.UUID are examples of custom field types. There are many different custom field types—and you can make your own—but you typically only need to use them for special cases.

Ecto types map to native types in the database that you use. A single Ecto type can map to multiple different native types. For example: varchar, string, and text PostgreSQL types are all handled by Ecto's :string type.

The field/3 function also accepts various options.[11] The most common option is :default, which lets you specify the default value for the column when null values are written or read from the database.

Another common option is :virtual. Use virtual fields when you want to attach custom data to a struct. You can add data to a virtual field either in Elixir—using Map.put/3—or from database queries.

Fields and associations go hand-in-hand. Let's take a look at associations next.

Schema Associations

Ecto schemas support one-to-one, one-to-many, and many-to-many associations. These association types have largely been standardized across database frameworks, so they will feel familiar. Here's how each type works:

One-to-One

The belongs_to/3 function defines a relationship that's either one-to-one or one-to-many. You use belongs_to/3 in the schema that contains the ID of the relationship. In our example, the SmsMessage schema includes a contact_id field.

The other side of the relationship uses the has_one/3 function to define the complete relationship.

One-to-Many

This type of relationship is similar to one-to-one, but the other side of the relationship uses has_many/3 to define the complete relationship.

---

10. https://hexdocs.pm/ecto/Ecto.Schema.html#module-types-and-casting
11. https://hexdocs.pm/ecto/Ecto.Schema.html#field/3

Many-to-Many

This is an advanced relationship type that's implemented using a third table. For example, we could implement a third table called ContactMessage that holds both contact_id and sms_message_id columns. This third table acts as a join table between the associated schemas. This would be helpful to implement a feature like group chats, where the one-to-many relationship type doesn't work.

The many_to_many/3 function is used to define this relationship type. This function requires a third table, which can either be another schema or a database table name.

Each association can be customized with a variety of options. You can control the relationship field names (these default to association_name_id), customize the type (Ecto.UUID instead of integer IDs), and more. The documentation for each function lays out all of the options available to you.

Ecto's documentation has a cheatsheet[12] that shows all of the various association types, how to define them, and how to update them.

Let's finish this section by completing the other side of the contact relationship.

Write the Contact Schema

Create lib/phone_app/conversations/schema/contact.ex and add the following code to it:

```
phone_app/lib/phone_app/conversations/schema/contact.ex
defmodule PhoneApp.Conversations.Schema.Contact do
  use Ecto.Schema

  @timestamps_opts [type: :utc_datetime_usec]
  schema "contacts" do
    has_many :sms_messages, PhoneApp.Conversations.Schema.SmsMessage

    field :phone_number, :string
    field :name, :string

    timestamps()
  end
end
```

This looks similar to the SmsMessage schema, but we use the has_many/2 function to define the other side of the association.

Once you add this schema, your project will compile without warning about the broken association. We'll use this schema in the rest of this chapter. First, we need to create our database tables.

---

12. https://hexdocs.pm/ecto/associations.html

Use Migrations to Create Database Tables

We have two schemas in our app, but we don't have corresponding database tables yet. Luckily for us, Ecto includes migration support out of the box. This will feel similar to ActiveRecord migrations, so you'll quickly be comfortable if you've used those before.

Migrations are scripts that modify your database. They are often used to add tables, add or modify columns, add indices, and so forth. You can even use migrations to update the data in your database, but this is an advanced case that we won't cover in this book.

Let's look at the basics of migrations and then define migrations for our two schemas.

Migration Basics

Ecto.Migration is implemented in a child library of Ecto called ecto_sql. This library contains all of the SQL-specific aspects of Ecto because Ecto isn't tied to a single database technology.

We'll cover a few of the key migration functions, but the migration documentation[13] goes into great detail for all available functions. The "Phoenix: Ecto Migrations Cheatsheet"[14] is useful as it covers all of the main patterns you'll use in migrations.

Often, multiple migration functions will be combined together. For example, the code create table(:widgets) do / end uses the create/2 and table/1 functions to create a new table, and create index(:widgets, [:name]) uses create/1 with index/2 to create a new index. The most commonly used functions are:

create table(:name) do / end
> Creates a database table with the fields added in the do block.

add :field_name, :field_type
> Adds a field to the database table. This can only be used inside of a create table block.

modify :field_name, :field_type
> Edits an existing field, such as changing the type or nullability of the field. This can only be used inside of an alter table block.

---

13. https://hexdocs.pm/ecto_sql/Ecto.Migration.html
14. https://devhints.io/phoenix-migrations

create index(:table_name, [:field_one, :field_two])

Creates an index on the specified table and field names. Additionally, create unique_index is used to define a unique index.

We'll use all of these in our migration. Let's do that next.

Define Our Migrations

Ecto provides a generator that creates a new schema file. When you run it, it will create an empty migration file. We'll run it twice, one for each database table:

```
$ mix ecto.gen.migration CreateSmsMessages
* creating priv/repo/migrations/20230507184727_create_sms_messages.exs

$ mix ecto.gen.migration CreateContacts
* creating priv/repo/migrations/20230507184731_create_contacts.exs
```

This format is exactly like ActiveRecord migrations: the current time is prepended to the name of the migration. This generator differs from ActiveRecord because you can't specify columns and tables in it. The previously mentioned mix phx.gen.schema generator does offer this feature, but we won't use it in this book.

Fill out the CreateSmsMessages migration with the following code (note that the file name will differ from yours):

```
phone_app/priv/repo/migrations/20230507184727_create_sms_messages.exs
defmodule PhoneApp.Repo.Migrations.CreateSmsMessages do
  use Ecto.Migration

  def change do
    create table(:sms_messages) do
      add :contact_id, :integer, null: false

      add :message_sid, :text, null: false
      add :account_sid, :text, null: false

      add :body, :text, null: false
      add :from, :text, null: false
      add :to, :text, null: false

      add :status, :text, null: false
      add :direction, :text, null: false

      timestamps(type: :utc_datetime_usec)
    end

    create index(:sms_messages, [:contact_id])
    create unique_index(:sms_messages, [:message_sid])
  end
end
```

And fill out the CreateContacts migration with the following code:

```
phone_app/priv/repo/migrations/20230507184731_create_contacts.exs
defmodule PhoneApp.Repo.Migrations.CreateContacts do
  use Ecto.Migration

  def change do
    create table(:contacts) do
      add :phone_number, :text, null: false
      add :name, :text

      timestamps(type: :utc_datetime_usec)
    end

    create unique_index(:contacts, [:phone_number])
  end
end
```

A migration consists of either a single change/0 function or the combination of up/0 and down/0 functions. Ecto runs the correct function based on whether we are migrating forward or rolling back a migration. Similar to ActiveRecord migrations, some operations are "reversible" and others are one-way. For example, create table can be reversed by dropping the table. But if we were to modify a column, then it would only be reversible if we provided the function with the original column definition.

The migration files are fairly self-explanatory. The great part of the migration DSL is that it's easy to read—it's inspired by the ActiveRecord migration format. All of the fields in our schemas are represented in the migration, with a PostgreSQL type that corresponds to the Ecto schema field type.

Finally, run your migrations with the command line migrator:

```
$ mix ecto.migrate
15:06:04.213 [info] == Running...CreateSmsMessages.change/0 forward
15:06:04.217 [info] create table sms_messages
15:06:04.228 [info] create index sms_messages_contact_id_index
15:06:04.231 [info] create index sms_messages_message_sid_index
15:06:04.236 [info] == Migrated 20230507184727 in 0.0s

15:06:04.274 [info] == Running...CreateContacts.change/0 forward
15:06:04.274 [info] create table contacts
15:06:04.279 [info] create index contacts_phone_number_index
15:06:04.281 [info] == Migrated 20230507184731 in 0.0s
```

We now have our schema and corresponding (empty) database tables. Before we move on, we're going to look quickly at the dangers of migrations.

Be Careful with Migrations

Migrations are inherently risky—this applies to Ecto, ActiveRecord, and any other migration framework. The risk comes from the fact that we're changing the schema of a running database. There's nothing that's stopping us from running drop table(:something_important) and losing all of our data, so we need to be careful with migrations.

The Fly.io blog post[15] about safe migrations can help you understand the risk that you face, and it offers tips for how to mitigate that risk. You can get away without knowing these dangers if you have a small amount of data, but a database with more data and throughput increases the migration risk.

One final note on this topic is that—similar to ActiveRecord—Ecto migrations have built-in protections to ensure that your database doesn't end up in an invalid state. The first protection is a DDL transaction that runs around the entire migration file. This transaction ensures that if an error occurs during different statements in our migration file, then the entire migration is rolled back and the database is unaffected. The second protection is a migration lock that's taken out on the schema_migrations table. This ensures that two migrations are not executed at the same time, which increases the chance for errors to occur.

You can disable these locks for certain operations, but you should rarely need to worry about them. They are there for protection, so disable them only when absolutely necessary. The most common operation that requires disabling them is when you add an index with the concurrently: true option.

Next, let's look at how to persist data in our database.

Use Changesets to Persist Data

Now that we have schemas, we need a way to insert data into the database. The approach that Ecto takes is significantly different than ActiveRecord, but it's one of the most loved components of Ecto. Let's dive into Ecto changesets.

Ecto.Changeset[16] lets us turn data parameters into a persisted database record. Changesets are used for creating new records or updating existing records. We can also validate incoming data using changesets—this ensures our database records match our application's business rules.

Let's write our first changeset. We'll start with the Contact schema because it has fewer fields.

---

15. https://fly.io/phoenix-files/safe-ecto-migrations/
16. https://hexdocs.pm/ecto/Ecto.Changeset.html

Create Our First Changeset

The functional nature of Elixir is visibly seen in the changeset function we're going to write. Changesets are built up over multiple function calls, which is perfect for the pipeline operator. This is usually done over several stages:

1. Cast the provided attributes to the types of our schema fields.
2. Apply validations on a per-attribute basis.
3. Define unique constraints on the schema.

Add the following code to the bottom of the Schema.Contact module:

```
phone_app/lib/phone_app/conversations/schema/contact.ex
import Ecto.Changeset

def changeset(attrs) do
  fields = [:phone_number]

  %__MODULE__{}
  |> cast(attrs, fields)
  |> validate_required(fields)
  |> unique_constraint([:phone_number])
end
```

Our code starts by importing the Ecto.Changeset module. This allows us to call changeset functions (like cast/3) without typing out the full module name.

Our changeset/1 function consists of a functional pipeline that calls various Ecto.Changeset functions. We start by calling cast/3 with three arguments: an empty schema struct, the input attributes, and the fields that we want to set in the database.

We pass an empty struct because cast/3 is capable of accepting structs with data, which is used to update a record. Passing an empty struct tells the changeset that we want to create a new record.

We call validate_required/2 to set our fields as required. This ensures that a null or empty :phone_number field will cause the changeset to fail. This is one of the many validation functions that Ecto.Changeset implements.

Finally, we call unique_constraint/2 to add information about field uniqueness. The unique_constraint function adds information about the constraint to the changeset, but it doesn't make any database queries. When we insert the changeset in the database, it will intelligently return an error if this constraint is violated.

The fields variable in this code is a convenience that has become my go-to pattern. It's important that required fields are properly defined, so it's convenient to start with code that says "everything is required" and then remove fields that aren't required using:

```
|> validate_required(fields -- [:non_required_field_name])
```

All of our fields are required, so we don't remove any fields here. Our schema does have a "name" field on it, but we're not updating that in this changeset, so we don't refer to it.

We'll use this changeset in a moment, but let's create the SmsMessage changeset next.

Create SmsMessage Changesets

We're going to define two different changesets for the SmsMessage schema. We'll use different changesets when we create a new SmsMessage versus when we update an existing SmsMessage. Add these functions to the bottom of the Schema.SmsMessage module:

```
phone_app/lib/phone_app/conversations/schema/sms_message.ex
import Ecto.Changeset

def changeset(attrs) do
  fields = [
    :contact_id, :message_sid, :account_sid, :body,
    :from, :to, :status, :direction
  ]

  %__MODULE__{}
  |> cast(attrs, fields)
  |> validate_required(fields)
  |> unique_constraint([:message_sid])
end

def update_changeset(attrs, struct = %__MODULE__{}) do
  fields = [:status]

  struct
  |> cast(attrs, fields)
  |> validate_required(fields)
end
```

Ecto doesn't require specific names for the changeset functions—they can be named anything we want. But you'll often see these function names because they clearly label how the changesets are intended to be used.

Use Our Changesets

We use the changeset functions by passing in input parameters. The return value of the functions is an Ecto.Changeset struct that includes the source data, any changes to the data, and whether the changeset is valid or not. Start an IEx session to try it out:

```
$ iex -S mix
iex> alias PhoneApp.Conversations.Schema.Contact
iex> Contact.changeset(%{})
#Ecto.Changeset<
  action: nil,
  changes: %{},
  errors: [phone_number: {"can't be blank", [validation: :required]}],
  data: #PhoneApp.Conversations.Schema.Contact<>,
  valid?: false
>

iex> Contact.changeset(%{phone_number: "x"})
#Ecto.Changeset<
  action: nil,
  changes: %{phone_number: "x"},
  errors: [],
  data: #PhoneApp.Conversations.Schema.Contact<>,
  valid?: true
>
```

We could write a validation function to guarantee that the phone_number field is a valid E.164 formatted number, but that would be overkill for this project.

Try out the SmsMessage changeset as well. The update_changeset/2 function requires that we pass a %SmsMessage{} struct in—this would be the existing data we're updating:

```
iex> alias PhoneApp.Conversations.Schema.SmsMessage
iex> struct = %SmsMessage{status: "test"}
iex> SmsMessage.update_changeset(%{}, struct)
#Ecto.Changeset<action: nil, changes: %{}, errors: [],
 data: #PhoneApp.Conversations.Schema.SmsMessage<>, valid?: true>

iex> SmsMessage.update_changeset(%{status: ""}, struct)
#Ecto.Changeset<errors: [status: {"can't be blank", []}], valid?: false>
```

The last response is truncated, but the main point is that the combination of the input struct and the parameters determines the changeset validity. When we pass in a struct that has :status set, the changeset is valid. But when we pass in the same struct and try to clear the :status field, it's no longer valid.

We'll use these changesets to create our data layer next.

Query Data with Ecto.Query

Ecto provides robust query functions—you can write most queries without writing SQL by hand. And if you run into a query that can't be written with the Ecto query language, you can safely use handwritten SQL.

We're going to build our data layer—everything needed to query and persist data in our application. The functions and patterns we use will be explained along the way. But first, we need to go over a module that we're going to use many times in this section.

The Repo Module

The generator that we used to create our application included an important (and simple) module. The PhoneApp.Repo module is how we'll handle all interactions with the database. The module is only one line of code:

```
phone_app/lib/phone_app/repo.ex
defmodule PhoneApp.Repo do
  use Ecto.Repo,
    otp_app: :phone_app,
    adapter: Ecto.Adapters.Postgres
end
```

The single line of code in this module—use Ecto.Repo—defines a bunch of functions. It includes functions to insert data, update data, make queries, execute raw SQL statements, and more. These functions could be customized by overriding them, but that's an advanced technique that you won't commonly need.

The Repo module is a core part of Ecto's design. Every single query in our application goes through our Repo. A Repo connects to a single database, so most applications have a single Repo module, but there's nothing stopping us from having multiple Repos that connect to different databases.

Let's use the PhoneApp.Repo module to make some queries!

Query and Persist Contacts

Our application will interact with Schema.Contact in a simple way. We only need to be able to retrieve a contact by its ID and create a new contact using a unique phone number.

There are many different ways we could organize the queries for our application. The approach used in this book is by no means the definitive way, but it's something that has served me well in small and scaled applications. To get started, create a file located at lib/phone_app/conversations/query/contact_store.ex and add the following code:

phone_app/lib/phone_app/conversations/query/contact_store.ex
```
defmodule PhoneApp.Conversations.Query.ContactStore do
  alias PhoneApp.Repo
  alias PhoneApp.Conversations.Schema.Contact
end
```

We'll use these aliases throughout our module. Let's add the first function to fetch a contact by its id:

phone_app/lib/phone_app/conversations/query/contact_store.ex
```
def get_contact!(id) do
  Repo.get!(Contact, id)
end
```

This function uses the PhoneApp.Repo.get!/2 function to retrieve an instance of the specified schema module by its primary key. If a record can't be found, an error will be raised. Try it out:

```
$ iex -S mix
iex> iex(9)> PhoneApp.Conversations.Query.ContactStore.get_contact!(1)
** (Ecto.NoResultsError) expected at least one result but got none in query:

from c0 in PhoneApp.Conversations.Schema.Contact,
  where: c0.id == ^1
```

If we were to use PhoneApp.Repo.get/2 instead, we would receive a nil response. The ! in the function name communicates that the function will raise an error. This pattern is idiomatic in Ruby and ActiveRecord, so it should feel familiar.

The next code is a bit more complex. Type it out, and then we'll walk through it:

phone_app/lib/phone_app/conversations/query/contact_store.ex
```
Line 1  def upsert_contact(%{from: from, to: to, direction: direction}) do
          contact_number =
            case direction do
              :incoming -> from
      5       :outgoing -> to
            end

          cs = Contact.changeset(%{phone_number: contact_number})

      10  Repo.insert(
            cs,
            returning: true,
            on_conflict: {:replace, [:updated_at]},
            conflict_target: [:phone_number]
      15  )
        end
```

The case on line 2 is necessary to determine the phone number of the contact based on whether an SMS message is incoming or outgoing. This is purely an application-level concern that will make sense when we write the SmsMessageStore.

The Contact.changeset/1 function is used on line 8 to create a changeset for our contact record. Then, that changeset is inserted into the database on line 10.

The function Repo.insert/2 is called with options that tell Ecto what to do if a duplicate contact occurs. This happens when a contact with the phone number already exists and the unique constraint is violated.

The insert pattern in this example is called an upsert (update or insert) and is natively supported by PostgreSQL and other databases. It's a bit complex with many different options and strategies for dealing with the uniqueness conflict. Ecto has great documentation[17] that goes through many different scenarios and outcomes.

Let's write the Query.SmsMessageStore next.

Query and Persist SMS Messages

We'll do more advanced things in the SmsMessageStore. Our store needs to insert new SMS messages, update the status of existing messages, return messages for a given contact, and load a list of messages for the sidebar view. We'll start with the create function because it's similar to what we just used in the ContactStore.

Create lib/phone_app/conversations/query/sms_message_store.ex and add the following code:

```
phone_app/lib/phone_app/conversations/query/sms_message_store.ex
defmodule PhoneApp.Conversations.Query.SmsMessageStore do
  import Ecto.Query

  alias PhoneApp.Repo
  alias PhoneApp.Conversations.Schema.SmsMessage
  alias PhoneApp.Conversations.Query.ContactStore
end
```

These aliases remove the need for us to type long module paths through our module. The line import Ecto.Query is new. We'll come back to this when we write a query. For now, add the create function:

---

17. https://hexdocs.pm/ecto/Ecto.Repo.html#c:insert/2-upserts

phone_app/lib/phone_app/conversations/query/sms_message_store.ex
```
def create_sms_message(params) do
  {:ok, contact} = ContactStore.upsert_contact(params)

  params
  |> Map.merge(%{contact_id: contact.id})
  |> SmsMessage.changeset()
  |> Repo.insert()
end
```

The first line retrieves the contact from the database so that we can pass its id field into our changeset.

This pattern for a create function is very useful: start with the provided parameters, overwrite (merge) any fields that the caller doesn't need to provide, turn it into the appropriate changeset, and then call Repo.insert/1 with that changeset.

When you use this pattern, you get the opportunity to overwrite the values of the params argument. In our case, we find or create the associated contact, so we fill out the contact_id in the changeset parameters.

Next, let's write a function that updates an existing SMS message. This is necessary because we'll track the external status of the message as it flows through the SMS network. Add the following code:

phone_app/lib/phone_app/conversations/query/sms_message_store.ex
```
def update_sms_message(message_sid, update_params) do
  case Repo.get_by(SmsMessage, message_sid: message_sid) do
    nil ->
      {:error, :not_found}

    existing ->
      update_params
      |> SmsMessage.update_changeset(existing)
      |> Repo.update()
  end
end
```

This function starts by calling Repo.get_by/2. This function looks up a schema by fields other than its primary key. In our case, we look up by a single field (message_sid), but we could look up by multiple fields.

We need to look up the associated schema so that we can call update_changeset/2 with it. Ecto is smart enough to know which fields have changed, and it sends only changed fields to PostgreSQL.

We could use Repo.update_all/3[18] to directly send an UPDATE statement to the database. update_all is useful in situations where you want to update in a single operation, but it's a best practice to update with a changeset. This forces your application to verify that the user has access to the record being updated, and you'll receive a copy of the updated struct from the Repo.update/1 function.

We have the persistence functions we need for SMS messages, so let's move on to querying for data. We'll be using Ecto's query builder DSL for this.

Association Functions

The Ecto.Changeset module exposes put_assoc/4 and cast_assoc/3 for interacting with associations, but they are optional. When you use these functions, Ecto detects changes in the association data and will insert or update those database records.

I find that casting associations as regular fields—like we did with contact_id—removes a layer of magic and is much simpler to understand. So I don't use the association changeset functions.

Use Ecto.Query for More Advanced Queries

Ecto.Query[19] provides a query builder DSL that gives you complete control over your database queries. Ecto queries end up feeling like SQL, but they have extra protection that comes from Elixir's compile-time guarantees.

Ecto knows about our application schemas because they are defined in code. It uses this knowledge to verify that we're querying columns that exist and that they are aliased correctly. Ecto uses macros and compile-time checks to guarantee that any data sent to the database has been properly sanitized. In the end, we get a familiar syntax with extra safety!

Let's ease into Ecto.Query with a simple function that loads all messages with a given contact. Add this to the bottom of SmsMessageStore:

---

18. https://hexdocs.pm/ecto/Ecto.Repo.html#c:update_all/3
19. https://hexdocs.pm/ecto/Ecto.Query.html

phone_app/lib/phone_app/conversations/query/sms_message_store.ex
```
def load_messages_with(contact) do
  from(
    m in SmsMessage,
    where: m.contact_id == ^contact.id,
    order_by: [desc: m.inserted_at],
    preload: [:contact]
  )
  |> Repo.all()
end
```

This sure does feel a lot like SQL! The close connection to SQL makes it easy to convert handwritten queries into an application.

Our code works because of the import Ecto.Query function at the top of this module. Typically, you'll use this import anytime your code calls the Ecto.Query.from/2 function.

Let's break apart this query. The code m in SmsMessage tells the query builder that we are assigning the schema SmsMessage to the variable m. We use this to reference columns on the table. Then, where: m.contact_id == ^contact.id filters the query based on the contact_id column equaling the value of contact.id.

The caret symbol (^) is used to insert the contact's id value into the query. Don't confuse this with the pin operator (^) that we used in pattern matching. It's just the symbol that Ecto's authors chose to use.

The order_by: [desc: m.inserted_at] line sorts our query by the inserted_at column. Finally, preload: [:contact] tells Ecto that we want it to load the contact association. This works similarly to ActiveRecord, where an additional query is made to load all of the contact associations.

Also like ActiveRecord, we have the choice to join the contact association into our query and preload it without any additional queries. You don't need to type out the following code, but here's what it would look like to join in the contact and preload using the join data:

phone_app/lib/phone_app/conversations/query/sms_message_store.ex
```
def example_load_messages_with_join(contact) do
  from(
    m in SmsMessage,
    join: c in assoc(m, :contact),
    where: m.contact_id == ^contact.id,
    order_by: [desc: m.inserted_at],
    preload: [contact: c]
  )
  |> Repo.all()
end
```

Once the from function is closed, nothing has happened. If you pipe into IO.inspect here, you will see an Ecto.Query struct but no data. We tell Ecto to execute this query using the Repo.all/1 function.

Let's add one more query that's a bit more complex. Type this out at the end of the module:

phone_app/lib/phone_app/conversations/query/sms_message_store.ex

```elixir
def load_message_list do
  distinct_query =
    from(
      m in SmsMessage,
      select: m.id,
      distinct: [m.contact_id],
      order_by: [desc: m.inserted_at]
    )

  from(
    m in SmsMessage,
    where: m.id in subquery(distinct_query),
    order_by: [desc: m.inserted_at],
    preload: [:contact]
  )
  |> Repo.all()
end
```

At a glance, this query looks a lot more complex, but upon closer inspection, it's similar to what you just wrote. There are a few additional keywords that we'll break down.

The line select: m.id results in the SELECT statement generated by Ecto to contain only this one field. This is necessary in our subquery because we only care about comparing the id field. Ecto has a lot of flexibility with how you can use select:. You can use it to append virtual fields to your query, select data into different data structures, and more.

The usage of distinct: [m.contact_id] is exactly what it looks like. This adds a DISTINCT ON clause to the query so that the contact_id field is unique.

This subquery efficiently loads the sidebar view so that only the most recent message for each contact appears. It gets pulled in with where: m.id in subquery(distinct_query). (Of course, you can do this in ActiveRecord as well.)

One benefit of Ecto's query builder DSL is its readability. There's very little magic here. We write queries that are obvious in their functionality at a glance, but we also benefit from Ecto's security and helper functions. There's a bit of a learning curve because so many different options are available, but the Ecto.Query documentation[20] is very comprehensive.

And with this, our SmsMessageStore is complete! We could stop here and use the store module in our application, but there's a code organization technique that helps create clarity. Let's create a context to wrap our functions.

Put Everything in a Context

Code organization has been and always will be a hot topic. People have many different opinions. Whether right or wrong, these opinions tend to solidify into best practices based on the community's preference. A code organization technique called "contexts" has taken hold in the Elixir community.

Let's break down what contexts are and then create one of our own.

What Is a Context?

Although they can be intimidating at first, contexts are simple. They are modules that group together related functions. This grouping is typically done based on the domain of the application you're building—which means you get to decide the context boundaries.

Contexts define a public API between different parts of your application. This makes it harder for spaghetti code to pop up in your app because the callable functions are clearly available in the context module. This context module is typically one level below your main application module prefix.

In our PhoneApp application, we'll create a context module called PhoneApp.Conversations. This module holds all of the functions that can be used by other parts of the application (like Phoenix Controllers, which we'll cover in the next chapter.)

There's nothing stopping other parts of the application from reaching in and "violating" the context boundary. It's more like an agreement to not do so.

The biggest obstacle for developers starting out with contexts is "what should I put in my context module?" The best answer is to make a decision with the information you have on hand and don't sweat the details too much. You can always change the context as needed. And you don't need to strictly follow the context rules—nothing prevents you from making the best decision for your app.

_____

20. https://hexdocs.pm/ecto/Ecto.Query.html#content

Create PhoneApp.Conversations Context

Contexts are entirely opinion-based, so we're going to cover a technique that has worked well for me personally. This technique uses a combination of delegated functions and regular functions to create a context. Delegated functions live in another module (like our store modules defining database operations) and are supported out of the box in Elixir with defdelegate. Let's use it to create delegates for many of our store functions.

Create lib/phone_app/conversations/conversations.ex with the following code:

```
phone_app/lib/phone_app/conversations/conversations.ex
defmodule PhoneApp.Conversations do
  alias PhoneApp.Conversations.Query
  alias PhoneApp.Conversations.Schema

  defdelegate get_contact!(id), to: Query.ContactStore

  defdelegate create_sms_message(params), to: Query.SmsMessageStore
  defdelegate update_sms_message(sid, params), to: Query.SmsMessageStore
end
```

defdelegate/2 is an incredibly useful function. It defines a function on the module that calls a function in another module. (You can customize the function name if they don't match.) This lets us write our query code in an isolated module and then export it to the rest of the app in the context.

You may have noticed that this context doesn't include the data-loading functions that we wrote in our store. This is because we're going to improve on the API of these functions by wrapping them in a struct.

Create lib/phone_app/conversations/schema/conversation.ex with the following code:

```
phone_app/lib/phone_app/conversations/schema/conversation.ex
defmodule PhoneApp.Conversations.Schema.Conversation do
  @enforce_keys [:contact, :messages]
  defstruct @enforce_keys
end
```

This is a struct that requires contact and messages fields to be provided. This is added to the schema folder—even though it's not an Ecto schema—because it serves a role as part of our application's data structure.

Go back to the PhoneApp.Conversations context module and add these functions to the bottom:

```
phone_app/lib/phone_app/conversations/conversations.ex
def load_conversation_list do
  messages = Query.SmsMessageStore.load_message_list()
```

```
  Enum.map(messages, fn message ->
    %Schema.Conversation{
      contact: message.contact,
      messages: [message]
    }
  end)
end

def load_conversation_with(contact) do
  messages = Query.SmsMessageStore.load_messages_with(contact)
  %Schema.Conversation{contact: contact, messages: messages}
end
```

These functions use the queries that we wrote earlier, but they each wrap the result in a helpful Conversation struct. This is entirely optional, but it leads to a nicer function for the rest of the application.

And that's it for our application's query layer! We aren't actually doing anything with it yet, but the next chapter pulls everything together to make our application take shape.

Wrapping Up

Ecto is a library for data mapping and database queries. It takes a different design approach than Ruby's ActiveRecord library, but somehow it ends up feeling familiar. Many of the concepts and terms are similar between the libraries, so you'll be right at home as you learn to use it. Ecto is used to query the database, translate data into your application, and change data from your application.

Ecto schemas are modules that define your application's data structure. Ecto uses a schema to know how to map data from the database into an Elixir struct. You can define associations in your Ecto schema, such as one-to-one, one-to-many, and many-to-many associations. These associations are standardized across database libraries, so they feel identical to ActiveRecord associations.

Migrations are used to create your database tables, fields, and indices. Ecto has a robust data migration format that's similar to ActiveRecord migrations. But you have to be careful with migrations. Anytime that you change the structure of a database, you run the risk of causing problems in your application or with your database performance. These risks exist in any migration library, so they aren't an Ecto issue. There are best practices that you can follow to reduce the risks.

Ecto changesets are used to insert or update data, and they are significantly different than the approach ActiveRecord takes. Changesets really highlight the functional nature of Elixir. Changesets are built over several function calls: start with the source data, cast input parameters to the right format, and validate that the data is in a valid format. Once you have a valid changeset, you use Repo.insert or Repo.update to persist the data to the database.

Every application needs to query data from a database. Ecto provides some helpful functions like Repo.get_by that quickly find data in the database. But you often need to write custom queries with advanced filters, joins, and ordering. The Ecto.Query module provides a complete query DSL that feels a bit like SQL. Ecto.Query is integrated into the Elixir language, so it feels natural to use. And it knows about your Ecto schemas, so it can verify that fields exist and are in the correct format.

Finally, you created a context module to expose the public functions of our application. Contexts are useful to organize your application into distinct groupings. But don't sweat the details of contexts too much. Make the best decision for your application contexts based on the information you have at the moment, but remember that you can easily change a context over time.

We'll use this chapter's queries and data in the next chapter. We'll create an API and interface for our application using the Phoenix framework. Things will take shape rapidly, so get ready!

## CHAPTER 7

Serving Requests with Phoenix

Phoenix is the biggest name in the Elixir ecosystem. If you've heard of Elixir before this book, there's a high chance that you've heard about Phoenix or Phoenix LiveView. We can't cover everything that Phoenix can do in a single chapter, but you'll learn enough to be dangerous with it.

Phoenix is a web-development framework that uses the Model-View-Controller (MVC) design pattern. It's well-integrated into the Elixir ecosystem primarily due to it being the most widely used framework in Elixir. On the surface, it's similar to Ruby on Rails, but it's fundamentally different in its goals and philosophy.

We'll go over the basics of Phoenix in this chapter. You'll serve web requests with controllers, use an asset pipeline for static assets, and learn about components for a clean UI. We'll use the Ecto-based data layer that we wrote in the previous chapter in order to read and write data.

Finally, we'll finish the chapter by looking at what else Phoenix can do. Phoenix's primary use case is web requests, but there are other offerings such as Phoenix Channels, Phoenix LiveView, and the authentication generator. We won't go deep into these topics, but you can continue learning about them in the official docs.

Let's start by going over what Phoenix is and how it compares to Rails!

Explore the Foundations of Phoenix

Phoenix is Elixir's most popular web-development framework. On the surface, this seems like it would be a large library with a ton of code, but it's actually fairly lightweight. (As of writing this paragraph, there are 46 files in the main lib/phoenix folder of the project.) This simplicity means that it's relatively quick to learn how to effectively use Phoenix to write web applications.

The differences between Rails and Phoenix are numerous—they are different frameworks, have different goals, and are built for different programming paradigms! Instead of attempting to list specific differences, this section covers major differences in the goals and development of each framework.

We're covering as much of Phoenix in this chapter as we can, but there's a dedicated book if you want more. Check out *Programming Phoenix 1.4 [TV19]* by Chris McCord (Phoenix's creator), Bruce Tate, and José Valim.

Let's first look at how Phoenix can work with so little code, and then we'll compare Phoenix and Rails. Let's get started!

What Is Phoenix?

Phoenix is a fairly lightweight library, but it has a ton of features. This is due to the core Phoenix library integrating with other libraries to achieve key features. You won't often interface with these other libraries directly, but it's important to know about them in case something goes wrong or you need to change a setting.

Here are the features that Phoenix brings to the table, either directly or through integrations with other libraries:

Serve Web Requests via Controller Modules
Serving web requests is the core feature of Phoenix. Phoenix interfaces with the Plug[1] library to make this possible. Plug consists of a pipeline that lets you modify a web request via composable middleware modules. This is similar to how Rack[2] works in Ruby.

Provide HTML Helpers, Templates, and Components
Phoenix provides the Phoenix.HTML[3] package for HTML-related helper modules. Phoenix also provides a component framework[4] via the phoenix_live_view package, so you can easily convert frontend code into components and use them across your application. Phoenix components are becoming more prominent, and they will likely replace Phoenix.HTML in the future.

Integrate with a Web Server That Works out of the Box
Phoenix doesn't provide a web server, but it uses Bandit[5] instead. Bandit is a pure-Elixir web server that's built for high concurrency and safety.

---

1.   https://hexdocs.pm/plug/readme.html
2.   https://github.com/rack/rack
3.   https://github.com/phoenixframework/phoenix_html
4.   https://hexdocs.pm/phoenix_live_view/Phoenix.Component.html
5.   https://github.com/mtrudel/bandit

Previously, a pure-Erlang web server called Cowboy[6] was the default web server.

Integrate with Ecto to Provide Data Access

Ecto works well with Phoenix. The Phoenix/Ecto[7] package integrates Ecto changesets and structures into Phoenix's form helpers. This creates a seamless experience when using Ecto changesets in Phoenix controllers and views.

Provide Real-Time Foundations

Phoenix provides the foundation for creating real-time web applications via Channels. Phoenix provides WebSocket support as well as helpers that make it easy to write real-time applications. The Phoenix LiveView[8] package takes this a step further with server-rendered real-time HTML.

You may have noticed something: these features are all web-request related. There's no mailer, job system, database, or storage code found in Phoenix. This highlights a fundamental difference between Rails and Phoenix. Let's dig into that.

External Web Servers

BEAM-based web servers are scalable enough to use without a proxy in front of them. It's a common pattern in many other languages (including Ruby) to use a proxy (nginx, Apache, and so on) that can handle a large amount of concurrent connections. This is due to concurrency limitations in Ruby and other languages.

Due to the BEAM's concurrency model, it's possible to run a production-grade web application without a proxy in front of it. This simplifies deployments without sacrificing safety.

How Does Phoenix Compare to Rails?

It has been a goal from the beginning of Rails that "Rails is omakase."[9] Omakase means "I leave the details up to you," so Rails intends to provide all of the features needed to create a high-quality application. Ruby has a rich gem ecosystem, but Rails has absorbed and recreated popular gems into the framework itself. The all-in-one nature of Rails—and how the framework

---

6.   https://github.com/ninenines/cowboy
7.   https://hexdocs.pm/phoenix_ecto/main.html
8.   https://github.com/phoenixframework/phoenix_live_view
9.   https://dhh.dk/2012/rails-is-omakase.html

actually extends parts of the language itself—leads to a distinction in the Ruby community between "Ruby developers" and "Rails developers."

This philosophy is entirely different in Phoenix.[10] Phoenix aims to be a high-quality web framework. It provides a relatively minimal set of web-oriented features (listed in the previous section) that have a specific focus. If you want to do things it doesn't offer, it encourages you to pull in external libraries to solve those goals.

A big difference between Rails and Phoenix is the amount of "magic" in each. Magic refers to things that work in a particular way, but it's difficult to trace how exactly they work. This is also known as implicit behavior.

Rails is full of magic. This feels great in many ways, but it becomes difficult to debug problems as your application scales. Phoenix avoids magic. Whenever possible, things are done explicitly and in a way that you can trace more easily. As an example, look at how each framework handles HTTP middleware. Rails implicitly loads a default set of middleware that can be confusing to find and modify. Phoenix lists all of the middleware in MyAppWeb.Endpoint, so you can quickly see exactly what is running and in what order.

This chapter isn't meant to come across as "Phoenix is better than Rails." It's meant to highlight some of the differences between them so that you can decide what's best for yourself. On the surface, they share a lot of similarities, but the differences run deep and are often based on differences of opinion.

Before we can get started actually working with Phoenix, you'll need to make sure your code is ready.

Prep Your Project

We'll continue the project started in the previous chapter. Some of the code that we need to write is tedious and isn't well-suited for a book. Instead, you can copy the code from the online code listings into your project.

Book Source Code

 The source code for this book can be found in its zip file on the PragProg website.[11] When you extract this zip file, you'll receive a code directory with subfolders under it.

---

10. https://dockyard.com/blog/2015/11/18/phoenix-is-not-rails

11. https://media.pragprog.com/titles/sbelixir/code/sbelixir-code.zip

Execute the following commands to copy important files over. The prefix code refers to the folder you just downloaded. Run this in the `phone_app` project folder that you started in the previous chapter.

```
$ cp code/phone_app/priv/repo/seeds.exs priv/repo/seeds.exs
$ cp code/phone_app/priv/repo/delete_seeds.exs priv/repo/delete_seeds.exs
$ cp code/phone_app/lib/phone_app_web/components/layouts/app.html.heex
    lib/phone_app_web/components/layouts/app.html.heex
$ cp -R code/phone_app/lib/phone_app_web/controllers/message_html
      lib/phone_app_web/controllers
$ cp code/phone_app/lib/phone_app/conversations/schema/new_message.ex
    lib/phone_app/conversations/schema/new_message.ex
```

Add the following dependencies to mix.exs at the end of the deps/0 function and then run mix deps.get:

```
phone_app/mix.exs
{:ex_phone_number, "~> 0.3"},
{:faker, "~> 0.17", only: [:dev, :test]},
```

Run the seeds.exs script that you just grabbed from the code listing. A "seed script" is a script that sets up test data for local use. Our script creates records for 500 different SMS messages between 20 different phone numbers.

At this point, you should be able to start the app with minimum warnings:

```
$ mix run priv/repo/delete_seeds.exs
$ mix run priv/repo/seeds.exs
```

You'll see warnings about missing routes at this point. We'll fix those up throughout the chapter.

Port 4004 Instead of 4000

Update your config/dev.exs file to point to port 4004 instead of 4000:

```
phone_app/config/dev.exs
config :phone_app, PhoneAppWeb.Endpoint,
  http: [ip: {127, 0, 0, 1}, port: 4004],
```

This change will remove potential headaches where your application is running on the default port that may already be in use. The rest of this book will assume port 4004 for all requests.

Let's finally get started with Phoenix. We'll start by looking at the request lifecycle, and then we'll write our controller.

Route Requests Through Phoenix

As requests come into an application, it's important that they get sent to the right function in your application. Along the way, they'll get transformed and interacted with by middleware functions. Middleware can serve any purpose, but you'll often write middleware to set common data and validate that the request can be served.

Phoenix uses the Plug[12] library, which refers to middleware as "plugs." Plugs can be either functions or modules.

Let's look at how Phoenix encapsulates plugs inside of the Phoenix.Endpoint module. Once we get these basics down, we'll move on to our controller.

How Requests Flow

The Phoenix generator creates several files as part of its generation process. These files relate to one of three things: your application code that lives in PhoneApp, your web-specific code that lives in PhoneAppWeb, or the configuration files. The App and AppWeb namespaces are best practices that encourage separation and clarity between your application logic and web logic.

One of the files that the Phoenix generator created—when you ran mix phx.new in Chapter 6—is called PhoneAppWeb.Endpoint. An Endpoint[13] manages the request lifecycle for any requests sent to it. (By default, your application has a single endpoint, but you can actually mount multiple endpoints on different ports.)

Our PhoneAppWeb.Endpoint module found at lib/phone_app_web/endpoint.ex has about 50 lines of code that outline exactly what happens in our application request lifecycle. The basic shell looks like this:

```
phone_app/lib/phone_app_web/endpoint.ex
defmodule PhoneAppWeb.Endpoint do
  use Phoenix.Endpoint, otp_app: :phone_app

  # ... Many lines outlining your application's request flow
end
```

The line use Phoenix.Endpoint brings in all of the functionality needed for this module to be an endpoint. This file has many more lines, but we won't go through each one. Instead, here's the most important section:

---

12. https://hexdocs.pm/plug/Plug.html
13. https://hexdocs.pm/phoenix/Phoenix.Endpoint.html

```
phone_app/lib/phone_app_web/endpoint.ex
plug Plug.MethodOverride
plug Plug.Head
plug Plug.Session, @session_options
plug PhoneAppWeb.Router
```

The plug function is used to define the middleware that each request goes through. You don't need to worry about all of the default plugs that Phoenix includes, but you can always view the source or remove the plug from the endpoint if needed. There are no magic (implicit) plugs in your application—only what you see in this file.

The line plug PhoneAppWeb.Router passes a request through our application-specific routing code. Let's dive into this module.

Routing Basics

Phoenix and Rails both use a central router to dispatch a request to the correct handler. These routers use a similar scheme to each other, so they feel familiar.

The Phoenix generator created the PhoneAppWeb.Router module for us. This module serves as the central router for your application, and it comes with a few lines of code to help you get started:

```
phone_app/lib/phone_app_web/router.ex
defmodule PhoneAppWeb.Router do
  use PhoneAppWeb, :router

  pipeline :browser do
    plug :accepts, ["html"]
    plug :fetch_session
    plug :fetch_live_flash
    plug :put_root_layout, {PhoneAppWeb.Layouts, :root}
    plug :protect_from_forgery
    plug :put_secure_browser_headers
  end

  pipeline :api do
    plug :accepts, ["json"]
  end

  scope "/", PhoneAppWeb do
    pipe_through :browser

    get "/", PageController, :home
  end
end
```

The first line is a use function, but it looks a bit odd. Rather than using an external Phoenix module, it's using PhoneAppWeb. This pattern is used by

Phoenix's generator to help your application feel a bit cleaner. The generated code for this module uses a bit of dynamic programming, but we can see that the router function just uses and imports other modules:

```
phone_app/lib/phone_app_web.ex
defmodule PhoneAppWeb do
  # Phoenix uses dynamic programming to clean up the `use` function
  defmacro __using__(which) when is_atom(which) do
    apply(__MODULE__, which, [])
  end

  def router do
    quote do
      use Phoenix.Router, helpers: false

      # Import common connection and controller functions to use in pipelines
      import Plug.Conn
      import Phoenix.Controller
      import Phoenix.LiveView.Router
    end
  end
end
```

You'll see this pattern in most modules that use Phoenix modules—it keeps your application code cleaner.

Let's go back to our router. The pipeline function defines a set of plugs that a particular request will flow through. This lets you conditionally invoke middleware based on the route being called.

A pipeline is referenced with the pipe_through/1 function. If necessary, you can pipe through multiple pipelines, such as pipe_through [:api, :authenticated].

The scope function is used to group a collection of routes together. The way that you scope your requests will depend on your application but is often done based on different authentication needs or URL grouping.

The line get "/", PageController, :home defines a handler for requests to GET /. A request will be sent to the PhoneAppWeb.PageController.home/2 function. There are other functions corresponding to different HTTP verbs, such as post, put, and delete.

In addition to individual HTTP verbs, you can use resources/4[14] to define a full suite of endpoints in one line. For example, the following line of code would produce the noted routes:

```
resources "/widgets", WidgetController
# The following routes are generated, viewable with `mix phx.routes`
```

---

14. https://hexdocs.pm/phoenix/Phoenix.Router.html#resources/4

```
GET      /widgets              PhoneAppWeb.WidgetController :index
GET      /widgets/:id/edit     PhoneAppWeb.WidgetController :edit
GET      /widgets/new          PhoneAppWeb.WidgetController :new
GET      /widgets/:id          PhoneAppWeb.WidgetController :show
POST     /widgets              PhoneAppWeb.WidgetController :create
PATCH    /widgets/:id          PhoneAppWeb.WidgetController :update
PUT      /widgets/:id          PhoneAppWeb.WidgetController :update
DELETE   /widgets/:id          PhoneAppWeb.WidgetController :delete
```

Notice that some of the routes have :id in them. This is a route parameter that will be passed to the controller action. All of this should feel familiar—routes are defined almost identically to how they are in Rails.

That's enough theory, let's get to code. We'll define our first route, create the controller and action, and render HTML via a template.

Serve Requests with Phoenix Controllers

Phoenix uses the Model-View-Controller (MVC) design pattern. MVC manifests in different ways depending on the framework and use case. MVC has three distinct parts. Models hold and operate on the data of the application. Views represent what the user sees and interacts with. Controllers accept input from a client and coordinate all of the important logic that's needed to serve a request. This all happens in a repetitive cycle as a user uses your application.

Rails uses this same pattern, so this should feel familiar. This pattern emerges naturally as you use Phoenix, so you don't need to worry about the details too much right now. As you proceed through the chapter, you'll see the separation between views, controllers, and your application logic. Let's jump right in and create a controller action.

Write Our First Controller Action

A good strategy to start a new endpoint is to work as the request flows. This means that we'll work from router, to controller, to data, and finally to views. This takes place over several modules across the entire application—everything works together to give us the final result. Add the following routes to the PhoneAppWeb.Router module:

```
phone_app/lib/phone_app_web/router.ex
scope "/", PhoneAppWeb do
  pipe_through :browser

  get "/messages", MessageController, :index
  get "/messages/new", MessageController, :new
  post "/messages/new", MessageController, :create
  get "/messages/:contact_id", MessageController, :show
end
```

Don't remove the default PageController route in your project—normally you would delete this route, but keep it so you don't get test failures in Chapter 10, Testing Elixir, on page 171.

We'll work through each of these four routes by the end of the chapter.

We could have used resources/4 for our routes, but it doesn't quite fit with the URL structure. So we use the longer form instead.

If you tried to start the app now, you would see many warnings about Message-Controller being undefined. Let's create that module and add our first action:

phone_app/lib/phone_app_web/controllers/message_controller.ex
```elixir
Line 1  defmodule PhoneAppWeb.MessageController do
   -      use PhoneAppWeb, :controller
   -
   -      plug :load_conversation_list
   5
   -      def index(conn, _params) do
   -        case conn.assigns.conversation_list do
   -          [%{contact: contact} | _] ->
   -            path = ~p(/messages/#{contact.id})
  10            redirect(conn, to: path)
   -
   -          [] ->
   -            redirect(conn, to: ~p(/messages/new))
   -        end
  15      end
   -
   -      defp load_conversation_list(conn, _params) do
   -        conversations = PhoneApp.Conversations.load_conversation_list()
   -        assign(conn, :conversation_list, conversations)
  20      end
   -   end
```

A lot is going on here, so let's break it all down. The first thing you'll notice is the use function on line 2. This is the same pattern that was used in the router earlier—it sets up the necessary code to make our controller work.

The plug on line 4 acts like a before_action filter in Rails. The load_conversation_list/2 function will be called for every action in this controller. Each page of this app has a sidebar that contains all conversations, so the plug ensures the data is always loaded.

The load_conversation_list/2 function calls the Conversations context module to load the conversation list. (You added these functions in the previous chapter.) assign/3 is used on line 19 to set this data in a special location called assigns. Assigns can be accessed in the conn struct—as on line 7—and in templates.

The index/2 function is called whenever the URL http://localhost:4004/messages is loaded. It's called with a Plug.Conn struct that includes everything about the request, and the params provided for the request. If the conversation list has a conversation, then the request will be routed by the redirect/2 function to the detail page for that message. If the conversation list doesn't have any messages, then the request will redirect to a form to send a new message.

The code path = ~p(/messages/#{contact.id}) uses an important concept called verified routes.[15] The ~p sigil verifies that the provided route is present in your application and can be used. It would emit a warning if you were to replace the path with ~p(/nope).

Start the app with iex -S mix phx.server and navigate to http://localhost:4004/messages. Your browser will redirect to the detail page. We haven't defined it yet, so Phoenix shows the error "function PhoneAppWeb.MessageController.show/2 is undefined or private." If you get redirected to /messages/new, make sure that you run the seed functions from the previous section.

Next, let's define the show action.

Serve HTML via a Controller Action

The show action will be the main view for our user interface. It will display the selected conversation and will present a form to send a new SMS message.

To achieve this behavior, our action will need to load the contact, load the conversation with that contact, and assign a changeset to power the form. Add the following code to the MessageController module:

```
phone_app/lib/phone_app_web/controllers/message_controller.ex
def show(conn, params = %{"contact_id" => contact_id}) do
  contact = PhoneApp.Conversations.get_contact!(contact_id)
  conversation = PhoneApp.Conversations.load_conversation_with(contact)

  conn
  |> assign(:conversation, conversation)
  |> assign(:changeset, changeset(params))
  |> render("show.html")
end

defp changeset(params) do
  conversation_params = Map.get(params, "message", %{})
  PhoneApp.Conversations.new_message_changeset(conversation_params)
end
```

---

15. https://hexdocs.pm/phoenix/routing.html#verified-routes

In addition, add the following line to the Conversations module:

```
phone_app/lib/phone_app/conversations/conversations.ex
defdelegate new_message_changeset(params),
  to: Schema.NewMessage,
  as: :changeset
```

The show function is fairly straightforward. We use the context functions to query for our data and to set up a changeset. (You copied the NewMessage module into the app earlier in this chapter.)

We won't cover the entire NewMessage changeset, but it follows a powerful pattern for forms:

```
phone_app/lib/phone_app/conversations/schema/new_message.ex
defmodule PhoneApp.Conversations.Schema.NewMessage do
  use Ecto.Schema
  import Ecto.Changeset

  embedded_schema do
    field :to, :string
    field :body, :string
  end

  def changeset(attrs) do
    fields = [:to, :body]
    attrs = force_country_code(attrs)

    %__MODULE__{}
    |> cast(attrs, fields)
    |> validate_required(fields)
    |> validate_change(:to, &validate_phone_number/2)
  end

  # ...data functions below
end
```

This schema and changeset don't write data to the database. They only validate data and turn it into a predictable format. The Phoenix form helpers know how to work with this data to create a form. It all fits together pretty seamlessly!

If you load the app at this point, you'll see an error that "no show html template defined for PhoneAppWeb.MessageHTML." We need to create a view that Phoenix can use to render HTML.

Create a file at phone_app_web/controllers/message_html.ex with the following contents:

```
phone_app/lib/phone_app_web/controllers/message_html.ex
defmodule PhoneAppWeb.MessageHTML do
  use PhoneAppWeb, :html

  embed_templates "message_html/*"
end
```

A bit of magic is going on here. Phoenix will use the PhoneAppWeb.MessageHTML module when the PhoneAppWeb.MessageController calls the render function. If the request was for JSON data, then PhoneAppWeb.MessageJSON would be used instead. This lets you build a single controller that responds to both HTML and JSON data through the relevant views. (This is similar to Rail's render method.)

The embed_templates/1 function tells the view to use external HTML templates. You can also use inline HTML with the ~H[16] sigil, but our views are large enough to warrant separate files. You'll see how to use ~H later in this chapter.

You already copied the .html.heex templates earlier in this chapter, so the views are already in your project.

Start your server with iex -S mix phx.server and load http://localhost:4004/messages. You'll see a list of conversations on the left-hand sidebar and a loaded conversation in the center, as in the following figure.

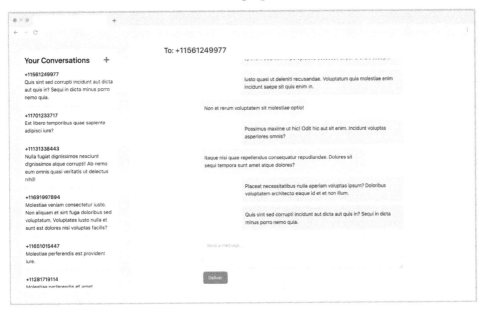

If you try to submit the form, you'll see it doesn't work. We'll add that next!

Take Action on User Input

We don't have a create action defined, so our form raises "function PhoneApp-Web.MessageController.create/2 is undefined or private" when we submit it.

---

16. https://hexdocs.pm/phoenix_live_view/Phoenix.Component.html#sigil_H/2

Let's create a basic action that creates an SMS message. (In the next chapter, we'll connect our app to a mock SMS server that sends and receives Twilio-compatible SMS messages.)

Add the following functions to the MessageController:

```
phone_app/lib/phone_app_web/controllers/message_controller.ex
def new(conn, params) do
  render(conn, "new.html", changeset: changeset(params))
end
```

```
phone_app/lib/phone_app_web/controllers/message_controller.ex
def create(conn, params) do
  create_changeset = changeset(params)

  case Ecto.Changeset.apply_action(create_changeset, :insert) do
    {:ok, message_params} ->
      case PhoneApp.Conversations.send_sms_message(message_params) do
        {:error, err} when is_bitstring(err) ->
          conn
          |> put_flash(:error, err)
          |> new(params)

        {:ok, _result} ->
          redirect(conn, to: ~p(/messages))
      end

    {:error, changeset} ->
      render(conn, "new.html", changeset: changeset)
  end
end
```

This function first checks if the NewMessage changeset is valid or not. This checks that the phone number is correct and that all fields are included correctly. If the parameters are valid, then the send_sms_message/1 context function is called.

The controller will either render the new.html template with errors, render new.html with a flash message, or redirect to the contact conversation.

Flash is the only concept we haven't talked about already. Flash messages[17] are session-persisted messages that display on the next page load. In our app, they are rendered in the layouts/app.html.heex file.

Our app doesn't have a send_sms_message/1 function. Let's add a mock version that persists to the database but doesn't actually send an SMS message.

---

17. https://hexdocs.pm/phoenix/controllers.html#flash-messages

phone_app/lib/phone_app/conversations/conversations.ex

```
def send_sms_message(params = %Schema.NewMessage{}) do
  # This version of send_sms_message uses mock data, it doesn't
  #   make an HTTP request.
  #
  # Later, we will write a new version that sends an HTTP request
  #   to a mock SMS server.
  params = %{
    message_sid: "mock-" <> Ecto.UUID.generate(),
    account_sid: "mock",
    body: params.body,
    from: "mock",
    to: params.to,
    status: "mock",
    direction: :outgoing
  }

  create_sms_message(params)
end
```

Nothing is exciting here. We're simply calling the create_sms_message/1 function with mock data. We'll fill this out in the next chapter!

Try to fill out the form with various messages. You'll see that they get added to the conversation you're in. You can also press the large plus button at the top left[18] to create a new contact. Attempt to send invalid messages as well. You can use invalid phone numbers, or submit a message consisting of only spaces. Everything should work, and errors are presented back to you when something goes wrong.

Let's switch gears and end this section by looking at how our web server is started.

How Does Our Server Start?

In this chapter, you started a web server with iex -S mix phx.server. It's easy to take this for granted, but it's useful to recognize why a server starts and what port it starts on.

Phoenix uses configuration files to set up certain parts of the framework. If you look at the config/dev.exs file, you'll see a line that tells Phoenix to configure a server on port 4004:

phone_app/config/dev.exs

```
config :phone_app, PhoneAppWeb.Endpoint,
  http: [ip: {127, 0, 0, 1}, port: 4004],
```

---

18. http://localhost:4004/messages/new

You could change this line to change the port that Phoenix dev environment runs on.

This configuration alone doesn't actually start a server. The `mix phx.server` command that we run has special instructions[19] that tell Phoenix to start a server. It looks something like this:

```
def run(args) do
  Application.put_env(:phoenix, :serve_endpoints, true, persistent: true)
  Mix.Tasks.Run.run(open_args(args) ++ run_args())
end
```

Because you have to explicitly tell Phoenix to start a server, one of the big mistakes that people make when deploying a Phoenix app isn't starting the server. This has largely been fixed by clearer documentation in the Phoenix deployment guides and generated code that configures it correctly. But keep an eye on this if you notice that your application is starting without a web server.

Let's briefly talk about bundling and serving static assets in Phoenix.

Manage Static Assets

Phoenix takes a hands-off approach to your asset pipeline. This lets you build and bundle your JavaScript, CSS, images, fonts, and other assets the way that you want to. It would be a bit cumbersome if there wasn't some way to manage assets out of the box, so the `phx.new` generator sets up a basic asset pipeline for you.

Phoenix 1.7 installs an esbuild-powered[20] asset pipeline. Esbuild is an asset bundler that's extremely fast and doesn't rely on external languages to be installed. It dramatically simplifies the development and deployment of assets when compared to Webpack-based pipelines.

The Phoenix generator also sets up Tailwind CSS[21] for you. Tailwind is a class-based CSS library that has become very popular. Tailwind lets you apply styles directly in your HTML instead of writing custom CSS. (I personally love Tailwind.)

The asset pipeline is configured inside of the `config.exs` file. You can see the relevant lines here—these are already in your project so you don't need to type anything out:

---

19. https://github.com/phoenixframework/phoenix/blob/v1.7.6/lib/mix/tasks/phx.server.ex
20. https://esbuild.github.io/
21. https://tailwindcss.com/

```
phone_app/config/config.exs
# Configure esbuild (the version is required)
config :esbuild,
  version: "0.17.11",
  default: [
    args:
      ~w(
        js/app.js
        --bundle
        --target=es2017
        --outdir=../priv/static/assets
        --external:/fonts/*
        --external:/images/*
      ),
    cd: Path.expand("../assets", __DIR__),
    env: %{"NODE_PATH" => Path.expand("../deps", __DIR__)}
  ]

# Configure tailwind (the version is required)
config :tailwind,
  version: "3.2.7",
  default: [
    args: ~w(
      --config=tailwind.config.js
      --input=css/app.css
      --output=../priv/static/assets/app.css
    ),
    cd: Path.expand("../assets", __DIR__)
  ]
```

Plus, the dev environment will automatically reload assets using watcher scripts:

```
phone_app/config/dev.exs
watchers: [
  esbuild:
    {Esbuild, :install_and_run, [:default, ~w(--sourcemap=inline --watch)]},

  tailwind:
    {Tailwind, :install_and_run, [:default, ~w(--watch)]}
]
```

You don't need to worry about changing these options until you have specific asset needs—they work great out of the box.

The most important part of the asset pipeline is the output directory. Phoenix expects to find assets in the priv/static/assets folder. The generator sets this up properly, but keep this in mind if you choose to use another asset pipeline tool like Webpack.

If you want to leverage esbuild plugins, or if you want to use something else, then follow the instructions in the Phoenix Asset Management docs.[22] You can also generate your Phoenix application to not include assets by changing the options passed to mix phx.new.[23]

When you are ready to ship to production, it's important to "digest" your assets. Digesting gives a unique hash to each file—based on its contents—so you can easily cache your assets. Your build pipeline should call mix phx.digest to achieve this, and Phoenix will include the correct files automatically. Asset instructions are included in the Phoenix deployment docs, so we won't go over it further in this chapter.

Let's switch over to a topic that's frontend-adjacent. We'll look at how to use components to clean up your frontend HTML code.

Use Components to Keep Your User Interface Clean

It's important to give your users consistent style and interaction across your application. Your buttons, modals, lists, tables, and so on should all feel like they belong together. This is done by using consistent CSS styles and JavaScript code across your frontend. You could do this by ensuring perfect HTML and CSS class usage across your application, but that's bound to have inconsistencies appear. Of course, Phoenix supports a better way—components.

Components are self-contained HTML templates, but they offer benefits over normal HTML. Components let you define the attributes that are required to use them, so you can be sure they're used in the proper way across your app. They can do a lot more, but we'll only go over their basics in this chapter.

Components are implemented in modules that include use Phoenix.Component. Similar to routers and controllers, the PhoneAppWeb module has a function that handles this for us. So, when you see use PhoneAppWeb, :html, know that it's pulling in Phoenix.Component.

You've already used a component without knowing it. The templates that you copied earlier in the chapter have a message_form component that defines the form used to send an SMS message. We'll take this message_form component and define the attributes that go into it. Then we'll create a few example components that are separate from our app.

Let's start by defining our attributes!

---

22. https://hexdocs.pm/phoenix/asset_management.html
23. https://hexdocs.pm/phoenix/Mix.Tasks.Phx.New.html

Component Attributes

Here's the MessageHTML module that we defined earlier in this chapter:

```
phone_app/lib/phone_app_web/controllers/message_html.ex
defmodule PhoneAppWeb.MessageHTML do
  use PhoneAppWeb, :html

  embed_templates "message_html/*"
end
```

The use of embed_templates automatically turns any templates in the folder into a component. We have an HTML file located at lib/phone_app_web/controllers/message_html/message_form.html.heex, so this makes a message_form component available for us to use.

We use this component like so:

```
phone_app/lib/phone_app_web/controllers/message_html/show.html.heex
<li class="w-full">
  <.message_form changeset={@changeset} contact={@conversation.contact} />
</li>
```

We also use it like so:

```
phone_app/lib/phone_app_web/controllers/message_html/new.html.heex
<div class="mt-4">
  <.message_form changeset={@changeset} contact={nil} />
</div>
```

These files were included with the files you copied in, so you have them in your project, but you may not have looked through them yet.

This component is pretty simple to use, but it would benefit from defining the attributes that can go into it. Let's do so by modifying the MessageHTML module:

```
phone_app/lib/phone_app_web/controllers/message_html.ex
# Define the attributes that go into the message_form component, located
# inside of the templates directory.
alias PhoneApp.Conversations

attr :changeset, Ecto.Changeset, required: true
attr :contact, Conversations.Schema.Contact, required: false, default: nil

def message_form(assigns)
```

Yes, this function head without a body is intentional! The Phoenix.Component code picks this up and associates the attributes to the correct component. This means that you can define multiple components inside of the same file.

Each attribute and its corresponding type are defined by the attr function. The type can either be a struct or one of a few predefined types such as :string, :integer, :any, or others.

In addition to the type of attribute, we can define whether it's required as well as a default value. Our form always requires an Ecto.Changeset struct, but the contact attribute is allowed to be nil. There are a few other attribute options[24] that you can use. These options serve as compile-time warnings and provide documentation.

If you start your application, you'll see that a warning now appears for the message_html/new.html.heex file:

```
warning: attribute "contact" in component
  PhoneAppWeb.MessageHTML.message_form/1 must be a
  {:struct, PhoneApp.Conversations.Schema.Contact}, got: nil

lib/phone_app_web/controllers/message_html/new.html.heex:6
```

To fix the warning, you can remove the contact: nil attribute from the noted line (new.html.heex:6).

We get this warning because we're passing nil in for a component that must be a Contact struct. This was accepted by the compiler before we defined the attribute as having a specific type. Once we define its type as a Contact struct, the compiler provides us with this helpful warning message.

The message_form component is about as basic as it gets. It takes a few known inputs and renders HTML based on them. But components can actually do more than that. Let's look at some of the more advanced features.

Advanced Component Features

Our app is pretty basic, so we don't have any complex components in it. But there are a few features that are useful as you're building out your component library: ~H sigil and slots.

The ~H sigil lets you embed the HTML for a component directly in an Elixir function. This is largely a matter of personal preference, but the embedded template style can be a bit easier to work with. To use it, you simply return an ~H wrapped string from your component function.

Here's a basic button component:

---

24. https://hexdocs.pm/phoenix_live_view/Phoenix.Component.html#attr/3

```
phone_app/lib/phone_app_web/controllers/message_html.ex
attr :type, :string, default: "button", values: ["button", "submit"]
attr :text, :string, required: true

def simple_button(assigns) do
  ~H"""
  <button
    type={@type}
    class="rounded border bg-white text-gray-700 px-4 py-2"
  >
    <%= @text %>
  </button>
  """
end
```

Everything inside of the ~H sigil will be rendered when we use the simple_component:

```
<.simple_button text="Deliver" type="submit" />
```

If we wanted to have HTML inside of our button, it wouldn't work with this implementation. We can use slots to create a better button interface:

```
phone_app/lib/phone_app_web/controllers/message_html.ex
attr :type, :string, default: "button", values: ["button", "submit"]
slot :inner_block, required: true

def slot_button(assigns) do
  ~H"""
  <button
    type={@type}
    class="rounded border bg-white text-gray-700 px-4 py-2"
  >
    <%= render_slot(@inner_block) %>
  </button>
  """
end
```

Now we can pass in HTML for the button contents:

```
<.slot_button type="submit">
  <strong>Strong Button!</strong>
</.slot_button>
```

This example uses the default slot called inner_block, but you can have as many slots as you want by naming the slot. Named slots let you create a component that consumes and renders multiple content areas. Slots can do even more, so make sure to check out the excellent docs.[25]

---

25. https://hexdocs.pm/phoenix_live_view/Phoenix.Component.html#module-slots

Core Components

Phoenix includes a (fairly large) module that creates a simple component system for you. You don't have to use this module, but it has several useful components inside of it.

Open up the PhoneAppWeb.CoreComponents module at lib/phone_app_web/components/core_components.ex and check it out. This module may be a bit intimidating if you're new to web development—don't worry too much about it in that case.

The message_form component uses the input component defined in CoreComponents. This component renders the styled input—handling different input types properly—and includes an error section when the form has invalid data.

We won't go over this file too much, but it's important to know that it's here. You can change this file to fit your application, or you can use it as a pattern for your own application components.

Before we wrap this chapter, let's go over a few aspects of Phoenix that didn't make it into this book's project.

Phoenix Is More Than Controllers

Phoenix isn't an all-in-one web framework, but it does more than just HTTP requests. This chapter focuses on controllers, views, and components because those are the foundations, but there's even more that you can do with Phoenix.

We'll briefly touch on a few different major features that Phoenix offers: authentication, Phoenix Channels, and LiveView.

Authentication Generator

There's a good chance your application will need to support registering users, logging in, logging out, and restricting access to routes. Phoenix solves this by offering a generator[26] that adds authentication code to your application.

All you have to do is type mix phx.gen.auth Accounts User users to create the user system inside of the Accounts context. This will create all of the schemas, migrations, mailers, controllers, and tests. (If you run this in the book project, make sure to back up the project first.)

The Phoenix generator creates an authentication system in your app, but there are other libraries that are more like Devise—Ruby's all-in-one authentication

---

26. https://hexdocs.pm/phoenix/mix_phx_gen_auth.html

library. The Pow[27] library gives you an integrated authentication solution that works quite well. (This is my personal authentication library of choice.)

Phoenix Channels

Real-time features have become a staple of the modern tech stack. Real-time applications push changes from the backend to the frontend so the updated data is available to users without them having to take action. This creates a seamless experience that can make an application feel polished and snappy.

Phoenix Channels[28] provide an out-of-the-box way to quickly add real-time features to your application. Channels are backed by Elixir's process model and use WebSockets to communicate in soft real-time between the frontend and backend.

My other book, *Real-Time Phoenix [Bus20]*, covers close to everything about channels. They come with their own complexities, but Phoenix's implementation is truly top-notch.

Phoenix LiveView

Phoenix LiveView[29] takes real-time applications to the next level. LiveView is built on top of channels to provide a new real-time programming model.

In LiveView, the server manages all of the HTML and state of your application. The server pushes the HTML to the client and ensures it's updated as the state changes on the server. Essentially, LiveView completely replaces controllers and a lot of JavaScript.

One of the great things about LiveView is that Phoenix templates and components work there. If you learn how to write templates and business logic with Phoenix Controllers, you can take everything you've learned and move it over to LiveView!

Make sure to check out *Programming Phoenix LiveView [TD24]* by Bruce Tate and Sophie DeBenedetto. It's the best book to get started with LiveView!

Wrapping Up

Phoenix is one of the main libraries for Elixir application development. Phoenix is a bit like Rails in that it is the most prominent library in the ecosystem, but it has a significantly different objective than Rails does. Rails seeks to be

---

27. https://github.com/pow-auth/pow
28. https://hexdocs.pm/phoenix/channels.html
29. https://hexdocs.pm/phoenix_live_view/welcome.html

everything you need to build web apps, but Phoenix focuses only on serving requests. Phoenix integrates with other key libraries—like Ecto—to create a seamless experience for Elixir web developers.

Requests flow through Phoenix in a similar way to Rails apps. Requests enter the application and run through an Endpoint module. The endpoint processes the request and eventually submits it to the Router module. Your application router will determine how the request should be processed and then will submit it to a Controller module. Finally, your controller executes the request and returns a result to the client. This entire process is explicit in Phoenix, so you can trace exactly how a request is handled by your application.

Controllers accept input from users and determine how to process a request. They coordinate with the rest of your application. It's most common to have controllers call into your application code to do things like read and write from the database. Once a controller has processed a request, it renders a response (HTML, JSON, or other formats) that's returned to the client. Often, view-modules (like MessageHTML) are used to render the correct HTML.

The frontend of large applications can quickly become unwieldy. Use Phoenix components to create self-contained components. You can optionally define the attributes that a component supports—this helps ensure you always call a component the right way, with attributes of the correct type. Phoenix comes with a CoreComponents module that defines many helpful components for quickly building an application.

Phoenix doesn't care too much about your asset pipeline, but it does come with an esbuild-powered pipeline that includes TailwindCSS. You can swap out the asset pipeline for any other system you prefer. But make sure to hash your assets properly and include your assets in the application-build process.

Phoenix provides some awesome libraries and features that we don't cover in this book. The authentication generator gives you an entire user-based authentication system in a few commands. Phoenix channels provide a foundation to create real-time enabled applications. Finally, Phoenix LiveView provides a totally new paradigm for web development with a real-time web framework that lives on the server.

Phoenix is one of the most important libraries, so you'll get familiar with it as you build more Elixir applications. One thing that it doesn't do is make outbound HTTP requests. In the next chapter, we'll explore how the Req library allows us to perform outbound HTTP requests in our app.

## CHAPTER 8

Outbound HTTP Requests with Req

Applications rarely exist in isolation. They use APIs (Application Programming Interfaces) to interact with other applications—whether internal or external—to achieve their value. Applications interact with each other in many different ways, but the most common form of interaction is an HTTP-based API. By the end of this chapter, you'll have what you need to make your own HTTP requests from Elixir.

On the surface, making HTTP requests seems like an easy problem to solve. We pick an HTTP request library, integrate it into our application, and then move on with our day. But the problem is a bit more complex than that. (Don't worry, the end result will be straightforward.)

HTTP clients in Elixir have been continually evolving and growing over the years. When compared to Ruby, you'll see a lot of different Elixir HTTP clients. This means that several options can fill our needs, and it can be a little bit confusing as to which library we should use. Libraries also sit at different levels of abstraction, so they have different purposes. But don't worry, we'll use a client that's great for all applications.

In this chapter, we'll look at several of the different HTTP clients that are out there. We'll settle on Req as our first-choice client, and you'll use it to implement an API in our SMS app. And along the way, we'll cover additional topics such as application configuration and secrets.

Let's look at the different HTTP clients that are available in the Elixir ecosystem.

Decide on Which HTTP Client to Use

HTTP clients in Elixir have a long history. Even before Elixir, there were Erlang clients that are still used to this day in Elixir apps. Knowing the whole history doesn't provide you with much benefit, but it will be helpful to understand the different abstraction levels that clients can sit on top of.

Once you understand that, we can take a look at the major players and where they sit. There isn't a single right answer in the end, but you'll have a solid grasp of why we pick Req as our preferred client.

The Various Levels of Abstraction

Let's walk through the different levels of abstraction from the lowest to the highest.

Sockets

At the lowest level, HTTP requests are made over sockets. These sockets usually speak TCP.

It's not common to interface with a raw socket. Erlang provides the :gen_tcp module to interact with raw sockets over TCP.

Socket Protocol

Sockets exchange packets back and forth, but they need a defined protocol to communicate effectively with each other. In an HTTP API, the HTTP/1 or HTTP/2 protocol will be used.

Socket protocols are usually implemented by libraries that serve as a foundation for other libraries. For example, the Postgrex[1] library implements the Postgres protocol on top of a TCP socket.

Pooled Connections

A socket is a single connection, but we need multiple, simultaneous connections to scale our application. Pooled connections use a socket protocol library and add connection pooling to it.

It's important to have a handle on connection pooling as you scale an application. If your pool is too small, then you won't be able to achieve the scalability you need. If your pool is too large, then you can send too many requests to another service and cause it to crash.

A non-HTTP example of this is the pooling library PgBouncer. This library only pools Postgres connections, but it's one of the most important tools for scaling Postgres to high throughput.

All-Included Libraries

At the highest level of abstraction, there are libraries that provide all of the bells and whistles you'll need when building your own application.

Simple libraries will provide minimal features but generally give you what you need to be successful. Extensible libraries give you options that you

---

1.   https://github.com/elixir-ecto/postgrex

can override, provide ways to extend the core functionality, and are generally easier to use in your applications.

Ecto is an example of an extensible library that sits at the highest level of abstraction. It sits on top of Postgrex for socket protocol and DBConnection for connection pooling.

The Major Players

Let's look at a few of the major HTTP client libraries. You'll see these names in the Elixir community, so it's important to know what they are and the different roles they fill.

The history of HTTP clients in Elixir actually starts with a familiar face: Erlang. Let's look at the clients:

:httpc

Erlang ships with an included HTTP client module called :httpc. It only supports HTTP/1.1 protocol—not HTTP/2—and is a bit cumbersome to use. The options needed to properly make SSL requests, for example, are complex to remember and use.

Because of its relative difficulty, :httpc isn't commonly used. You'll see it used by some low-level libraries that don't want to include an HTTP library dependency, but very rarely.

Hackney and HTTPoison

The hackney[2] library is an all-included library that lets you make HTTP requests in Erlang. This isn't commonly used directly in Elixir. Instead, HTTPoison[3] wraps it and provides a friendly interface.

In the past, there were some problems with Hackney's security defaults (particularly around SSL) that caused people to move away from it. Despite this, you'll see HTTPoison commonly used even today.

Mint

Mint[4] is a socket protocol library for HTTP/1 and HTTP/2. It was written by members of the Elixir core team (but it isn't maintained by the core team) to solve shortcomings with the existing low-level HTTP clients at the time. It provides a better foundation for higher-abstraction HTTP clients than :httpc does.

---

2. https://github.com/benoitc/hackney
3. https://github.com/edgurgel/httpoison
4. https://github.com/elixir-mint/mint

Mint serves as the foundation for other libraries with higher levels of abstraction, but you won't use this in applications.

Finch

Finch[5] provides connection pooling on top of Mint.

You could use this in an application, but it's more common to reach for the next level of abstraction. Despite this, Finch is very popular even for people using it directly.

Tesla

Tesla[6] is an everything-included Elixir HTTP client. It's based on a Ruby library called Faraday. Tesla features an extensible plugin system as well as provides implementations for common tasks.

Some people prefer Tesla's module-based configuration and test-mocking features.

Req

Req[7] is an everything-included Elixir HTTP client built on top of Finch. It features an extensible plugin system as well as provided implementations for many common tasks.

There are quite a few options here, especially compared to Ruby. Let's dig into that.

Compared to Ruby

Ruby has a few commonly used HTTP clients: HTTParty, Faraday, and http.rb. These clients have been around for some time and appear to be largely adopted by the community. So, it comes as a bit of a surprise that there are so many options in Elixir.

There are two potential reasons for this. The first is that Elixir's concurrency model means that it's necessary to have a firm grip on the concurrency of your HTTP client. For example, if you accidentally issue 500 queries to the same URL at the same time, you may find that the other side crashes. So, you'll see libraries focused on pooling control in Elixir. Ruby is less concurrent, so you won't have this same problem and developers don't have to create solutions for it.

---

5. https://github.com/sneako/finch
6. https://github.com/elixir-tesla/tesla
7. https://github.com/wojtekmach/req

Another potential reason for the difference in HTTP libraries is that there hasn't been a pure-Elixir HTTP client until recently. All of the previous clients were based on Erlang foundations. Mint, Finch, and Req are all pure-Elixir libraries, so the chance of these sticking as the go-to libraries is higher than if they were Erlang-based.

Next, let's talk about why we'll use Req in this book.

The Decision

We have only three real choices: HTTPoison, Req, or Tesla. The other choices are too low-level or aren't friendly enough for us to even consider.

We'll immediately remove HTTPoison from consideration because it's based on dated foundations when compared to Req or Tesla. However, HTTPoison is still used by many apps and is actually not a bad client.

Let's consider Tesla next. This book was originally written to use Tesla, but it was changed because Req appears to be the future of Elixir HTTP clients. Tesla and Req both use Finch as their default HTTP adapter, so it's only a matter of preference.

Req is relatively new when compared to Tesla, but it has more approval in the ecosystem and provides all of the features we need. It works securely out of the box, is easy to use, allows for creating client libraries, and supports a rich set of HTTP features. It's a great fit for this book, so we'll use it.

Now, let's set up and then use Req!

Prep Your Project for Req

We'll start off by setting up Req and the application configuration that we'll use throughout this section. Then, in the next section, we'll write our HTTP client and connect it to our existing app.

Let's make sure that your project is prepared for this chapter. We'll use a provided helper app called mock_server that implements a Twilio-compatible SMS API, so you need to have this downloaded to your local computer if you want to see it in action.

Prep Your Project

We'll continue the project that you developed in the previous chapter. It's best to continue your own project from start to finish, but you can start with a clean version of the code by working out of the phone_app_end_7 directory provided in the book source code.

Book Source Code

The source code for this book can be found in its zip file on the PragProg website.[8] When you extract this zip file, you'll receive a code directory with subfolders under it.

In addition, we'll be using the mock_server codebase throughout this chapter. This is included in the code directory downloaded from the PragProg website, so make sure you grab it. You can start it by navigating into the project and starting the mix server:

```
$ cd mock_server
$ mix setup
$ mix phx.server
[info] Mock SMS server is starting. Access at the specified URL below.
[info] Follow book instructions for basic auth setup.
      Credentials = (username:mock-key-sid, password:mock-key)
[info] Access MockServerWeb.Endpoint at http://localhost:4005
```

Keep this running throughout the chapter. Let's set up Req next.

Set Up Req and Config

To use Req, you need to add it to your mix.exs file. Add the :req dependency to the end of the deps/0 function and then run mix deps.get:

phone_app/mix.exs
```
{:req, "~> 0.4"},
```

Next, we need to specify a few configuration values that our code will use to authenticate the API request. We do this with Config, which is a module that Mix provides out of the box.

In Ruby, it would be common to have a .env file and load development secrets via that file. In Elixir, it's more common to rely on application config and to have a secret configuration file that isn't checked into version control.

For our app, you'll create a dev.secret.exs file. The contents of it aren't actually secret, but we're treating them as if they were real-life API keys. If this were a real project that was stored in version control, you would always want to make sure that your secret files aren't committed up. Treat them like you would a .env file in a Ruby app!

First, update your config/dev.exs file to reference the config/dev.secret.exs file:

phone_app/config/dev.exs
```
import_config "./dev.secret.exs"
```

Next, create config/dev.secret.exs with the following contents:

---

8.   https://media.pragprog.com/titles/sbelixir/code/sbelixir-code.zip

phone_app/config/dev.secret.exs

```
import Config

config :phone_app, :twilio,
  key_sid: "mock-key-sid",
  key_secret: "mock-key",
  account_sid: "mock-account",
  number: "+19998887777",
  base_url: "http://localhost:4005/2010-04-01"
```

These config values allow your app to communicate with and authenticate to the mock Twilio API that this book provides. You'll see how to access them in your app in the next section.

Use Req to Make Requests

Req is quite simple to use for a majority of cases. For example, you would call Req.get!("https://www.google.com") to fetch the Google home page. For more advanced use cases, Req can be customized to include custom headers, authentication, or anything that you need.

For our app, we'll take advantage of Req.new/1 to create an HTTP client that can be used against our API. Once we have that, we'll create a context module to use the API in our application. Let's dive in!

Implement API-Client Module

Create a file at lib/phone_app/twilio/api.ex and type the following code:

phone_app/lib/phone_app/twilio/api.ex

```
Line 1  defmodule PhoneApp.Twilio.Api do
   -      defp twilio_config do
   -        Application.fetch_env!(:phone_app, :twilio)
   -      end
   5
   -      def req_client(opts \\ []) do
   -        config = twilio_config()
   -        default_base_url = Keyword.fetch!(config, :base_url)
   -        base_url = Keyword.get(opts, :base_url, default_base_url)
  10        key_sid = Keyword.fetch!(config, :key_sid)
   -        key_secret = Keyword.fetch!(config, :key_secret)
   -        force_base_url = Process.get(:twilio_base_url) # testing helper
   -
   -        Req.new(
  15          base_url: force_base_url || base_url,
   -          auth: {:basic, "#{key_sid}:#{key_secret}"}
   -        )
   -      end
   -    end
```

The function Application.fetch_env!/2 on line 3 returns the values that you configured in the dev.secret.exs config file. Everything inside of your config files is available to your application, so it's straightforward to use for application configuration.

Our config is defined as a keyword list, so we use the Keyword module to access individual values. You'll see on line 9 that the base_url value can be overridden via a function parameter. This pattern is extremely useful for testing, as you can swap out the URL for a library like Bypass.[9]

Finally, we use Req.new/1 on line 14 to configure a base set of options for our HTTP client. This lets us make API calls without having to set the options on each individual request. You'll see how clean this makes our API functions.

Add the following functions to the top of the file:

```
phone_app/lib/phone_app/twilio/api.ex
Line 1  def get_sms_message!(params, client \\ req_client()) do
  -       %{account_sid: account, message_sid: id} = params

  -       Req.get!(client, url: "/Accounts/#{account}/Messages/#{id}.json")
  5     end

  -     def send_sms_message!(params, client \\ req_client()) do
  -       account_sid = Keyword.fetch!(twilio_config(), :account_sid)
  -       %{from: from, to: to, body: body} = params
  10      body = %{From: from, To: to, Body: body}

  -       url = "/Accounts/#{account_sid}/Messages.json"
  -       Req.post!(client, url: url, form: body)
  -     end
```

These functions make HTTP calls to our API. Req provides a set of common HTTP functions such as Req.get!/2, Req.post!/2, Req.put!/2, and so on. These functions are quite easy to use!

We pass the form option to Req.post! on line 13. This encodes the body as a URL-encoded form. We could use the json option instead, but the Twilio API requires the form encoding to be used.

There is one unusual bit of syntax that you haven't seen before. In both of our function heads, we define client \\ req_client(). This isn't a typo—Elixir's default function arguments can invoke other functions! Each time that the function is invoked without a client argument provided, the req_client/0 function is called and passed into the function.

We won't cover it in this book, but you can completely customize any step of the Req request lifecycle. You could swap out the HTTP library that it

---

9.   https://hexdocs.pm/bypass/Bypass.html

uses and add middleware that transforms requests or responses. It may not be needed in every app, but it's nice to have full control when you need it.

Next, let's connect this client module to our app.

Use the API Client in Your App

As usual, we're going to expose our functions inside of a context module. Create lib/phone_app/twilio/twilio.ex and add the following delegates:

phone_app/lib/phone_app/twilio/twilio.ex

```
defmodule PhoneApp.Twilio do
  defdelegate send_sms_message!(msg), to: PhoneApp.Twilio.Api
  defdelegate get_sms_message!(msg), to: PhoneApp.Twilio.Api
end
```

Now, we can replace the PhoneApp.Conversations.send_sms_message/1 to deliver a message using our SMS API. Replace the existing function in lib/phone_app/conversations/conversations.ex with the following code:

phone_app/lib/phone_app/conversations/conversations.ex

```
Line 1  def send_sms_message(params = %Schema.NewMessage{}) do
          msg = %{
            from: your_number(),
            to: params.to,
     5      body: params.body
          }

          case PhoneApp.Twilio.send_sms_message!(msg) do
            %{body: resp = %{}} ->
    10        params = %{
              message_sid: resp["sid"],
              account_sid: resp["account_sid"],
              body: resp["body"],
              from: resp["from"],
    15        to: resp["to"],
              status: resp["status"],
              direction: :outgoing
            }

    20      create_sms_message(params)

          %{body: %{"code" => _, "message" => err}} ->
            {:error, err}

    25      _err ->
            {:error, "Failed to send message"}
          end
        end
```

```
30  def your_number do
      twilio_config = Application.get_env(:phone_app, :twilio, [])
      Keyword.fetch!(twilio_config, :number)
    end
```

At this point, all of these lines of code should feel right at home to you.

Our function starts on line 2 by defining the parameters needed to deliver an SMS message. We invoke our SMS API context function on line 8, which sends a message over HTTP. Finally, we handle success on line 20 by persisting our SMS message to the database. And if we get errors along the way, we return those to the caller.

We're almost done with the code for this section. Let's make one more adjustment, and then you can try out your app!

See Your App in Action

An SMS app needs two parties to make a conversation. Because this is a mock API, you'll have to talk to yourself. The MockServer app includes a way to reply to messages, but it requires a new route to be created. Let's add that and then use it from end to end.

Create the Webhook Controller

Create lib/phone_app_web/controllers/webhook/twilio_controller.ex and add the following code:

phone_app/lib/phone_app_web/controllers/webhook/twilio_controller.ex
```
defmodule PhoneAppWeb.Webhook.TwilioController do
  use PhoneAppWeb, :controller

  def sms(conn, params) do
    persist_message(params)

    conn
    |> put_resp_content_type("text/xml")
    |> send_resp(200, incoming_sms_response())
  end

  defp persist_message(params) do
    message = %{
      message_sid: params["MessageSid"],
      account_sid: params["AccountSid"],
      body: params["Body"],
      from: params["From"],
      to: params["To"],
      status: params["SmsStatus"],
      direction: :incoming
    }
```

```
    PhoneApp.Conversations.create_sms_message(message)
  end

  defp incoming_sms_response do
    """
    <?xml version="1.0" encoding="UTF-8"?>
    <Response></Response>
    """
  end
end
```

This controller route receives a payload and then persists the received SMS message to the database. This is just like the other controllers that we created in the previous chapter, except it replies with an XML payload instead of JSON or HTML. (XML is the format that Twilio requires for webhook responses.)

In addition, you need to add this route to the PhoneAppWeb.Router module. Add the following code to lib/phone_app_web/router.ex:

```
phone_app/lib/phone_app_web/router.ex
scope "/webhook", PhoneAppWeb.Webhook do
  pipe_through [:api]

  post "/sms", TwilioController, :sms
end
```

This routes POST requests to /webhook/sms to the PhoneAppWeb.Webhook.TwilioController.sms/3 function.

Use the App

Start the PhoneApp project using mix phx.server. In addition, start the MockServer project—from earlier in this chapter—with the same command.

Open two different tabs in your browser. Load the first to http://localhost:4004/messages/new and the second to http://localhost:4005.

On the first tab (PhoneApp), you'll see the message form to deliver a new message. Enter your phone number and type a message. In the second tab (MockServer), you'll see the message appears instantly in the table. There is a "reply" button that lets you send a message in response.

We don't cover real-time in this book, so you have to refresh the PhoneApp page to see the response come through. However, the MockServer app is built using LiveView, so messages will instantly appear without a page refresh. You can see the potential here even if we didn't implement it in our own project. We won't dedicate a chapter to LiveView in this book, but we'll touch on it in the final chapter.

We're almost done with our app. In the next chapter, we'll use an asynchronous job to update the status of our SMS message, so that it doesn't say "queued" in the UI.

Wrapping Up

HTTP clients are relatively easy libraries to use, but a lot of complexity hides beneath the surface. The varying levels of abstraction can create a bit of confusion regarding which library you should use for your app. Libraries at the lower levels of abstraction (such as socket protocols or pooled connections) are usable but will usually leave you wishing that they had more features. Full-featured libraries such as Req and Tesla will provide a solid foundation for any app out there. It's largely a matter of preference, but we picked Req for our app.

It's easy to use Req to make HTTP requests, but you'll likely need a configuration that tells the system which URL domain to send requests to, which authentication to use, and so on. You can store all of your application-specific configuration inside of the config directory, which is automatically loaded into your application. You can even set up a secret configuration such as dev.secret.exs, which you would then exclude from version control.

Req provides top-level functions such as Req.post!/2 and Req.get!/1 that make it a breeze to issue HTTP requests. But you can wrap up commonly used options into a base configuration with the Req.new/1 function. Plus, if your app has more advanced needs, you can customize the entire request and response lifecycle of Req. We were able to use our Req-based API in the send_sms_message/1 function without changing the rest of our app because we initially built it in a mocked-out way in the previous chapter.

Our last application-oriented chapter is up next. We'll be looking at asynchronous jobs in Elixir and specifically diving into the Oban library.

## CHAPTER 9

Asynchronous Jobs with Oban

There's a major tool missing from your Elixir toolbox right now—asynchronous jobs. They are a critical component for scaling up an application. Elixir has big shoes to fill here because Ruby comes with one of the best asynchronous job libraries out there—Sidekiq.

In their most basic form, async jobs run small or large units of work in the background of your application. Once the user has submitted a request, we use async jobs to process additional tasks such as sending emails, performing calculations, or triggering application-specific workflows. With more advanced usage, async jobs are used to power complex business logic with concerns such as uniqueness constraints and rate-limiting.

The first reaction to async jobs that many new Elixirists have is: "don't we have everything we need with GenServer?" It's true that Elixir provides async capabilities out of the box, but libraries provide a lot of functionality that would be complex to build ourselves. We'll talk about one of these libraries—Oban—and some of its capabilities in this chapter.

We'll start by looking at the use cases and implementation concerns that async job libraries handle. You'll understand why job systems are useful and what the traits of a good job system are. Due to Elixir's process model, there are a few different options for how we could handle running async code. We'll go over the different options before finally settling on the Oban[1] library to implement a simple worker in our SMS app.

Let's start by diving into what async jobs are used for.

---

1.   https://hexdocs.pm/oban/Oban.html

Understand Async Job Systems

Async jobs simplify our application by letting us extract side effects out of the main path of our code. This can dramatically improve the performance of our application in a variety of situations. We don't have to worry about whether we should make the expensive HTTP call in our controller. We can simply fire a background job and let it process!

A good async job system will do much more than this. Complex tasks can be broken into subtasks and orchestrated to solve difficult problems with less code than if you built it yourself.

Let's start by looking at use cases for async jobs, followed by a litmus test for when to extract code into an async job. We'll finish this section by considering what makes a good job system.

Async Job Use Cases

Async jobs can be used for a variety of different tasks. On one hand, we have extremely simple tasks like sending emails. On the other, we can build entire data pipelines with fan-out fan-in style processing.

As you're reading these use cases, it's important to consider that async jobs execute as fast as they can, but they are not time-guaranteed. For example, we may expect that enqueuing an email will send it immediately, but the job system could be backed up and the email may take seconds, minutes, or even longer to process.

Let's break down some common use cases:

Send emails after a request (basic)
> Emails are commonly executed asynchronously because they (almost always) require sending requests to external systems to deliver. Those systems could be slow or experience an outage. If we're implementing a "new user signup flow," then we may want to immediately create the user in our database, but we'll be okay if the welcome email is delivered behind the scenes.

Inform another system of an operation (basic)
> An operation happens in our system, and we want to let another system know over an API. We could do that inside of the operation request itself, but we'd encounter the same potential problems as with sending an email. Making the request inside of an async job gives us a more stable and scalable solution.

Execute code at some point in the future (medium)

> We want to respond to an operation that happens in our system, but we want to do so minutes or hours in the future. We need to use an async job to schedule code to execute at that point in the future. This is called a scheduled job.

Optimize repeating task (advanced)

> An operation happens frequently in our system, and it results in an expensive operation that calculates a cache value. We could let it calculate as many times as the operation happens, but that would be wasteful because it occurs frequently. Instead, we can leverage a unique job that ensures the operation only occurs once every so often.

Robust data pipeline (advanced)

> We have a data pipeline that requires a batch of jobs to finish before the next step occurs. That step produces many more tasks, which have to complete before the final task occurs. This is called a workflow and is fairly complex to implement. Job systems can help us by allowing us to tap into existing abstractions to write this complex data pipeline.

These are only a few use cases for async jobs. There are so many possibilities, and you'll start seeing more of them once you get comfortable with an async job system.

Let's go over a litmus test that you can use to determine whether a piece of code is a good candidate for an async job.

Async Job Litmus Test

Consider the following questions when evaluating a piece of code to see if it can be made async:

Is this code inherently costly?

> Sending HTTP requests, interacting with SMTP servers, and processing data-intensive requests are all things that have an inherent cost to them. If you execute this type of code in the main controller, it can hold up the connection and prevent a response from being received by the user. Instead, consider extracting it into an async job and allow it to finish behind the scenes.

Is this code at a relatively-high risk of failure?

> Certain pieces of code are more likely to experience intermittent failures that have nothing to do with the operation itself. For example, sending an HTTP request to a service that's experiencing an outage

will result in that request failing. If we're able to extract this code into an async job, then we can retry it after the system has had a chance to recover.

Do we need to control this code's concurrency?

Elixir will let you run a lot of requests simultaneously. This is both a good and bad thing. Often, we need to throttle the amount of concurrency that can happen with a given piece of code. If we use an async job system, we have full control over the amount of concurrency.

Does this piece of code need to execute immediately, or can it wait a bit?

If the code must run as part of the request, then it will be difficult to make async. But if it's acceptable to happen after the fact, then we're free to extract it into an async job.

Does the job system have features that simplify my development process?

Job systems often offer more than just executing units of work. They provide features like uniqueness, workflow management, batching, and more. You can tap into these features to save massive amounts of time on certain problems.

It helps to know what your job system can do so you know what is a good fit for it!

Now that we've established when we need a job system, here's how to pick a good one.

Requirements of a Good Job System

Not all job systems are built the same. Some are simple and seek to solve a single problem—execute async jobs. Other job systems provide robust features that make them quite powerful by comparison. Truly great job systems will provide the advanced features you need, but they make basic operation so easy that anyone can use them. Sidekiq in Ruby is a great example of a great job system that pulls this off well.

Here are some things to consider when looking at a job system:

Is it audited?

We need to know whether a job failed or succeeded, its progress, and so on. We should be in control of how long we hold this audit for.

Is it modular?

Ideally, we won't need to update the code powering our job system. But it's helpful to be able to implement our own logic or feature for any uncommon use cases we may have.

Does it have the advanced features we want?

> You may be looking only for executing basic jobs, but what happens as your application grows? A great job system will provide features like uniqueness control, rate-limiting, retry management, scheduled jobs, and workflow lifecycles.
>
> (You may need to pay for some of these features, similar to Sidekiq's licensing model.)

Is it scalable?

> The best job systems give us a ton of scalability without a ton of ceremony. In Elixir, that means expertly leveraging OTP to give us full control over scalability.

Is it observable?

> We need to know what's happening in the job system. It should be observed by metrics that are deployed to an external logging system. Or it should have a dashboard so we can observe the current state of the system.

Does it support transactions (ideally, it should)?

> Transactions are one of the greatest benefits of using a database. Job systems that tap into this will be easier to integrate into our system and have fewer bugs. The most popular Ruby job system—Sidekiq—is Redis-based and doesn't support transactions.

With this list of what makes a good job system, let's look at our options in Elixir and pick the best path forward.

Explore Asynchronous Jobs in Elixir

You have several options for how you can approach asynchronous jobs in Elixir. This is due to Elixir's process model—we can build simple or complex job systems inside of our existing application. The number of available options can be a bit overwhelming when you first start, so we'll look at a few common options before settling on a generic one that works for many situations.

The following examples will use a made-up piece of code that we want to make asynchronous. You don't have to type this code anywhere; it's only an example. Our scenario is that we have an HTTP endpoint that receives a data payload. We want to persist the payload to our database, but we also want to enrich the payload with data from a third-party API.

Let's jump in.

Do Nothing

The first technique can be easy to overlook—we can simply do nothing. Our code would run inside of the HTTP endpoint and directly enrich the data. It might look like this:

```
def create(conn, params) do
  enriched = enrich_data_via_api!(params)
  data = DataStore.persist!(enriched)
  json(conn, %{id: data.id})
end
```

In this example, we fetch the enriched data and then persist it into the database. This approach has a few benefits. The enriched data is immediately available—so our application could use it right away. Plus, we've written the simplest code possible to solve our problem, so that's an advantage for code cleanliness.

However, we have some significant drawbacks to this approach. If the enrichment API is down, then our API call will fail. If the enrichment API is slow, then users will feel that slowness in our API. Plus, the server has a connection held up while this request processes. (This last drawback is less significant in Elixir because servers have large connection limits compared to Ruby.)

These drawbacks are fairly significant, so let's make the code asynchronous.

Use a Task Process

Elixir provides a module called Task[2] that lets us easily spawn short-lived, task-specific processes. You could do this yourself, of course, but the Task module greatly simplifies it. However, there are shortcomings with Task that make it not a great fit for a job system.

Here's what that could might look like:

```
def create(conn, params) do
  data = DataStore.persist!(params)

  Task.Supervisor.start_child(MyTaskSupervisor, fn ->
    enriched = enrich_data_via_api!(params)
    DataStore.update_enriched!(data, enriched)
  end)

  json(conn, %{id: data.id})
end
```

---

2.   https://hexdocs.pm/elixir/Task.html

In this code sample, data is persisted in its basic, unenriched form. Our task then enriches the data and updates the database record. We could have used the simpler Task.start/1 function, but we used Task.Supervisor.start_child/2 because it ensures that tasks are given time to complete when an application shuts down. This is important to consider because applications stop and start during deployments.

This approach makes the basic data available immediately, and the enriched data will be available after the enrichment period. Our app would feel fast while making this API call, so the experience would feel significantly better to the end user.

This approach has a few major problems that are so severe that I've regretted it every time I've used it. Our app will spawn as many tasks as it can. If our API is hit with a large throughput, then the downstream requests will be significant. We've given up control over the parallelism of our async code, which is a big drawback! We also have no bookkeeping of the request. What if the API crashes, or our app reboots while processing? We have no guarantees that this code will ever finish!

With these drawbacks in mind, let's look at the last approach.

Use Oban

Oban is an Elixir job processing library that uses Postgres (or SQLite3) for coordinating and managing jobs. Oban is most similar to GoodJob[3] and Sidekiq.[4]

Oban uses processes to isolate jobs and provides complete control over job concurrency. Each job executes inside of its own process, which is started and handled by an Oban queue process.

Oban doesn't have the same problems that Task does. Oban controls the amount of concurrency automatically, has complete bookkeeping of our jobs, and handles application crashes well.

It's easy to define an Oban worker. Here's what our code might look like if we used Oban:

---

3. https://github.com/bensheldon/good_job
4. https://github.com/sidekiq/sidekiq

```elixir
def create(conn, params) do
  data = DataStore.persist!(params)
  EnrichWorker.enqueue!(data, params)
  json(conn, %{id: data.id})
end

# Example of an Oban Worker

defmodule EnrichWorker do
  use Oban.Worker

  def enqueue!(data, params) do
    %{id: data.id, params: params}
    |> new()
    |> Oban.insert!()
  end

  def perform(%Oban.Job{args: %{"id" => data_id, "params" => params}}) do
    enriched = enrich_data_via_api!(params)
    DataStore.update_enriched!(data_id, enriched)
    :ok
  end
end
```

You can see from this example that Oban workers are modules that implement the perform/1 function and they use Oban.Worker. That's all you need to create an Oban worker. You don't need to know anything about the underlying process model to use it, but you benefit from OTP best practices without even thinking about it!

We need to consider the potential downsides of this approach. There is slightly more code than the alternatives, but it's actually quite reasonable. The biggest downside is that a Postgres row is inserted and processed for each job placed into the queue. You won't run into a problem with this unless you're processing a lot of jobs per second, but it's worth mentioning. (Later in this chapter, we'll talk about why Postgres is actually a great choice for a job system.)

Overall, Oban is an excellent choice for asynchronous jobs. If you're building a system and looking to run code asynchronously, save yourself the hassle and start with Oban.

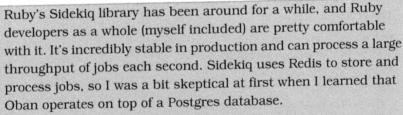

Oban vs. Sidekiq

Ruby's Sidekiq library has been around for a while, and Ruby developers as a whole (myself included) are pretty comfortable with it. It's incredibly stable in production and can process a large throughput of jobs each second. Sidekiq uses Redis to store and process jobs, so I was a bit skeptical at first when I learned that Oban operates on top of a Postgres database.

While there are differences in how Redis is operated versus Postgres, it's not difficult to use Oban at scale. Overall, the Elixir community's experience with Oban has proven that it's a stable job system that can process a large throughput of jobs. The added benefits of transactions and not needing to run a Redis server make it a compelling job system.

Next, let's implement an Oban worker in our SMS app.

Implement an Oban Worker

In the previous section, you got a sneak peek of what an Oban worker module looks like—it's really simple to create one. But before we get to that point, we need to set up Oban. Once Oban is set up for our app, we'll add our worker and test it out.

Add Oban to Our SMS App

Oban has great guides to walk you through implementing it. It's a fairly quick process, but it might change slightly over time as the library grows and changes. So if you do run into any issues, then make sure to read the Oban Installation Guide.[5]

The first step is to include the Oban dependency in mix.exs:

phone_app/mix.exs
```
{:oban, "~> 2.16"},
```

And then run mix deps.get to bring it into your project.

Oban uses a database to store jobs, so next you need to set up the migrations for it. Start by creating a new migration:

```
$ mix ecto.gen.migration add_oban_jobs_table
```

Then enter the following into the migration file. Your file name will vary because it's based on the time that you run the migration command:

---

5. https://hexdocs.pm/oban/installation.html

phone_app/priv/repo/migrations/20231112032011_add_oban_jobs_table.exs

```elixir
defmodule PhoneApp.Repo.Migrations.AddObanJobsTable do
  use Ecto.Migration

  def up do
    Oban.Migration.up(version: 11)
  end

  def down do
    Oban.Migration.down(version: 1)
  end
end
```

Then run mix ecto.migrate to run the migration.

This migration pattern puts all of the complex migrations behind an easy to use function. Plus, it makes it easy to handle future migrations as you keep Oban up-to-date over time.

Next, we need to add some configuration to set up our Oban queues. Add the following config block to config.exs:

phone_app/config/config.exs

```elixir
config :phone_app, Oban,
  repo: PhoneApp.Repo,
  plugins: [
    # 1 hour
    {Oban.Plugins.Pruner, max_age: 60 * 60}
  ],
  queues: [default: 10]
```

The important options of this configuration are queues and plugins. Queues are buckets that jobs fall into. A given queue has a certain amount of concurrency available to it—in our case, ten workers can execute simultaneously. (This number is per server, so three servers of ten workers would provide thirty concurrent workers across a cluster.) You can define as many queues as you want and however much concurrency you want.

Plugins extend the capabilities of Oban. The Pruner plugin removes completed jobs from the database—in our case, after one hour.

Let's also update the test.exs config so that you have control over jobs in the test environment:

phone_app/config/test.exs

```elixir
config :phone_app, Oban, testing: :manual
```

Finally, we need to add Oban to our application process list. Update the start function in lib/phone_app/application.ex to include the Oban Supervisor:

phone_app/lib/phone_app/application.ex

```
{Finch, name: PhoneApp.Finch},
{Oban, Application.fetch_env!(:phone_app, Oban)},
PhoneAppWeb.Endpoint
```

The order of entries in this list does matter. By placing Oban before our end-point—but after our Ecto repo, PubSub, and Finch—we ensure that our async jobs have access to the processes they need. Application supervision is too advanced of a topic for this book, but know that you have complete control over when processes start in your application.

You can verify that everything is working by checking the Oban config in your application. To do this, start an IEx session:

```
$ iex -S mix
iex> Oban.config()
%Oban.Config{
  ...
}
```

Now that Oban is in our app, let's create our worker!

Write an Oban Worker

Our SMS app has a problem when it's sending messages. Messages are not delivered instantly, so we need to keep track of the status of the message. Usually, SMS messages are delivered fairly quickly—within 10 seconds—but it's actually fairly common for SMS messages to run into issues during delivery. These issues can pop up minutes or hours after attempted delivery.

When we send a message, we'll use an async job to check the status of the message until it becomes finalized. The mock SMS server that's included with this book has a delay built in—up to 15 seconds—so we can test this flow out.

Let's start by creating a new worker module and an enqueue/1 function. Create lib/phone_app/conversations/worker/status_worker.ex and add the following code:

phone_app/lib/phone_app/conversations/worker/status_worker.ex

```
defmodule PhoneApp.Conversations.Worker.StatusWorker do
  use Oban.Worker

  alias PhoneApp.Conversations.Schema.SmsMessage

  def enqueue(%SmsMessage{} = message) do
    %{"id" => message.id}
    |> new()
    |> Oban.insert()
  end
end
```

The enqueue/1 function isn't standardized by Oban, but it provides a convenient way to enqueue jobs based on known arguments. In our case, an SmsMessage struct is turned into a set of parameters that's passed into the job.

Oban uses Ecto changesets and repo functions to insert jobs. The new/1 call turns arguments into an Oban.Job changeset, and then the call to Oban.insert/1 places that job in the database.

Arguments in Oban have similar limitations to Sidekiq. It's a best practice to only pass identifiers into the job arguments—as opposed to complex structs or maps—and load the data based on those identifiers in the job itself. Here's what that looks like when we write the perform/1 function:

```
phone_app/lib/phone_app/conversations/worker/status_worker.ex
alias PhoneApp.Conversations.Query.SmsMessageStore

def perform(%Oban.Job{args: %{"id" => message_id}}) do
  message = SmsMessageStore.get_sms_message!(message_id)
  %{body: resp} = PhoneApp.Twilio.get_sms_message!(message)

  case resp["status"] do
    "queued" ->
      {:error, "Message not ready"}

    status ->
      PhoneApp.Conversations.update_sms_message(
        message.message_sid,
        %{status: status}
      )
  end
end
```

This job follows a simple formula: load the data from the arguments, query the Twilio API for the current status, and then persist that status into the database. The perform/1 function can return a variety of possible results, which are all documented in the Oban documentation.[6] The update_sms_message/2 function returns either an ok or error tuple, so it works perfectly as a return value.

If we detect that the message still isn't ready, then we cause the job to fail and retry by returning {:error, reason}. Oban provides a default retry logic that's similar to Sidekiq—twenty retries over an exponential backoff period. (Like most things, you have complete control over the retry logic.)

If you tried to start this now, you'd get an error about SmsMessageStore.get_sms_message!/1 not existing. Let's add that quickly:

---

6.   https://hexdocs.pm/oban/Oban.Worker.html#t:result/0

```
phone_app/lib/phone_app/conversations/query/sms_message_store.ex
def get_sms_message!(id) do
  Repo.get!(SmsMessage, id)
end
```

We're almost done. Next, we'll integrate this job into the SMS creation flow.

Enqueue a Job After SMS Creation

Our job should be enqueued when an SMS message is created with certain properties (status = queued and direction = outgoing). We already have a create_sms_message/1 function that all SMS messages are created through, but it's a defdelegate. If we want to hook into it, we need to turn the defdelegate into a regular function.

In the lib/phone_app/conversations/conversations.ex file, delete the existing create_sms_message delegate and add the following function:

```
phone_app/lib/phone_app/conversations/conversations.ex
def create_sms_message(params) do
  PhoneApp.Repo.transaction(fn ->
    with {:ok, message} <- Query.SmsMessageStore.create_sms_message(params),
         {:ok, _} <- maybe_enqueue_status_worker(message) do
      message
    else
      {:error, cs} -> PhoneApp.Repo.rollback(cs)
    end
  end)
end

defp maybe_enqueue_status_worker(message) do
  case message do
    %{direction: :outgoing, status: "queued"} ->
      PhoneApp.Conversations.Worker.StatusWorker.enqueue(message)

    _ ->
      {:ok, :skipped}
  end
end
```

This function looks a little dense at first, so let's break it apart.

We start by wrapping the entire function body inside of Repo.transaction/1. This function wraps the provided function inside of a SQL transaction. If an error is raised or Repo.rollback/1 is called, the transaction rolls back and returns {:error, tuple}. If the function doesn't error, then the return value is wrapped in an {:ok, tuple}. This transaction is optional—you could insert the Oban job without one. However, it's usually important to guarantee that jobs are created alongside data.

We use a with statement to take advantage of the fact that our code follows a happy path. Each step must be successful, and any deviation from success should be rolled back. Our first step is to create the SMS message. After that, we enqueue a job only if the created message matches the format we want.

Last, we return the message variable. The Repo.transaction/1 function wraps it in an ok tuple, so our final result is transformed into {:ok, message}.

This code block highlights something important about Oban. Because it is a Postgres-backed job system, you can use transactions to guarantee that your job doesn't execute until the data and any other jobs are enqueued. In Ruby's Sidekiq library, you need to use after_transaction hooks or other techniques to only enqueue jobs after the transaction is finalized. With Oban, you don't have to think about it.

We've successfully added this job into our app, and we managed to do so without changing much code.

Our Worker in Action

Start your phone_app application and also the included mock_server application. Remember, you start each of them using mix phx.server. (If you need a reminder on how to use the mock_server application, refer to the previous chapter.)

Visit http://localhost:4004/messages and create a new SMS message. Then visit the mock server at http://localhost:4005/, and you'll see your message there. You can reply back from here as well.

Our SMS app initially says that the message is queued—you'll see this in the user interface. After a short time (up to 20 seconds or so) refresh the page and you'll see that "queued" has disappeared and our system is properly recognizing the message as delivered.

This status update happened because of our job. Without it, the message would appear to be queued forever, which would be rather confusing for users!

Our job is basic, let's quickly go over some of the more advanced features that Oban provides.

More About Oban

Oban is easy to get started with, plus it provides several features that make it a powerful part of an application. Some of these features are open-source, but there's even a paid version that adds a lot of advanced functionality.

We'll go over some of these features, although there are many more than we'll cover here. Let's start with the open-source features that you can use on the free version of Oban.

Telemetry (Open-Source)

Observability is a foundational requirement for a good job system. Oban uses a standardized library called Telemetry to let you decide which events you want to monitor.

All of Oban's telemetry events are documented in the Oban.Telemetry guide.[7] You can use these events to update stats systems such as Datadog or NewRelic. Here's an example of telemetry from one of my applications:

```
defmodule Super.Application do
  use Application

  def start(_type, _args) do
    events = [
      [:oban, :job, :start],
      [:oban, :job, :stop],
      [:oban, :job, :exception]
    ]

    :telemetry.attach_many("oban-logger", events,
                           &Super.ObanLogger.handle_event/4, [])
    # rest of application setup
  end
end

defmodule Super.ObanLogger do
  require Logger

  def handle_event([:oban, :job, :start], _measure, meta, _) do
    Logger.info("[Oban] started #{meta.worker}")
  end

  def handle_event([:oban, :job, event], measure, meta, _) do
    ms = ceil(measure.duration / 1_000_000)
    Logger.info("[Oban] #{event} #{meta.worker} ran in #{ms}ms")
  end
end
```

This is a basic example that only logs when jobs start, stop, or encounter an error. The important thing is that you have full insight into the job execution process.

---

7.   https://hexdocs.pm/oban/Oban.Telemetry.html

CRON Jobs (Open-Source)

Oban provides a CRON plugin[8] that makes it easy to run jobs on a repeating schedule. Repetitive tasks appear all the time in real-world systems, so Oban can save you some time.

Here's an example of the CRON format:

```
config :my_app, Oban,
  plugins: [
    {Oban.Plugins.Cron,
      crontab: [
        {"* * * * *", MyApp.MinuteWorker},
        {"0 0 * * *", MyApp.DailyWorker, max_attempts: 1},
        {"0 12 * * MON", MyApp.MondayWorker, queue: :scheduled},
      ]}
  ]
```

You have full control over when jobs execute, and you can customize their options such as the queue, number of retries, and so on.

Recover Stuck Jobs (Open-Source)

Jobs will only be removed from the system if they are fully processed—or if they fail enough times. However, it's common for a job to be executing while your application reboots or encounters an external problem (such as Kubernetes out-of-memory) that terminates it.

In these cases, the jobs will be stuck in an executing state that never goes away. Oban has a plugin to recover these stuck jobs, called Lifeline.[9]

This is a distinct advantage over the free-version Sidekiq library. In Sidekiq, a job that's processing while your application shuts down is lost. You can pay for Sidekiq Pro to solve this, but it works in Oban for free.

Web Interface (Paid)

Oban offers a web interface for a monthly fee. This is similar to Sidekiq's pro offering, although Oban's web interface isn't open-source. However, the fee supports the development of Oban. New features are regularly added, and the interface is kept up-to-date visually and feature-wise.

---

8. https://hexdocs.pm/oban/Oban.Plugins.Cron.html
9. https://hexdocs.pm/oban/Oban.Plugins.Lifeline.html

Pro Features (Paid)

For an additional monthly fee, Oban offers a robust set of pro features. You don't need these features to build your app, but they are useful once you hit a certain point or have an increased set of needs.

Some of the key pro features[10] include a more powerful execution engine, batched job support, strictly ordered job execution, and fan-in fan-out workflows.

Wrapping Up

If you're building an app, you will eventually need a solution to execute asynchronous jobs. There are many tasks that become simplified when executing them asynchronously, such as delivering emails, syncing data to other systems, or building a data pipeline to process your data. Reach for a job system if a piece of code has a high chance of failure, could be slow due to external factors, or benefits from concurrency.

Elixir provides all of the building blocks you need to write highly parallel systems, so you may be tempted to build your own solution to async jobs. For example, you could use Task or GenServer to process jobs in an async manner. Unless you have a really good reason not to, use an off-the-shelf library that provides a solid foundation such as controlled concurrency, transactions, and auditing.

Oban is the best job-processing library in the Elixir ecosystem. It's easy to get started with, but it offers many advanced features that let you grow your application over time. The best part about using Oban is that your application will follow best practices that have been laid out by the Oban developers. You'll be making good use of OTP and concurrency without even thinking about it!

The Oban worker you built in this chapter was a simple module that implemented a perform/1 function. You also added an enqueue/1 function to make it easy to add jobs to the Oban queue. Oban is backed by Postgres, so you were able to leverage transactions to guarantee that the data and job were inserted at the same time.

Before we wrap up our application, we need to write some tests. The next chapter will take us through tests for our entire application.

---

10. https://getoban.pro/docs/pro/overview.html

## CHAPTER 10

Testing Elixir

Tests are crucial for gaining confidence that your application works correctly and predictably. Love them or hate them, they remain important and necessary for professional software engineers. Elixir has an excellent built-in testing framework, which we'll cover in this chapter.

In the first chapter, you read that Elixir has a "culture of testing" that's similar to Ruby's culture of testing. But this is the first time we're mentioning tests! This doesn't mean that testing isn't important or should be an afterthought. Instead, it's a byproduct of how this book is structured—the previous chapters focused on how to use the library being shown. This dedicated testing chapter lets us cover techniques to test all of our libraries in one place.

We'll begin by testing our Ecto changesets. These tests won't have database or web requests in them, so they're as simple as they can get. Then, we'll cover other libraries that have been covered in this book: Ecto queries, external API requests, Phoenix requests, and Oban jobs.

By the end of this chapter, you'll be able to read and write Elixir tests. Plus, you'll have patterns to test each of the libraries included in this book. We won't be able to cover everything about testing—there's so much to it! Check out *Testing Elixir [LM21]* by Andrea Leopardi and Jeffrey Mathias for a full book on Elixir testing.

Let's write some tests!

Create Your First Test

Tests can get complex when the code you're testing includes dependencies or complex flows. So, we'll start simple and work our way up to more complex testing cases. But first, let's spend a little time comparing Ruby's testing ideas to Elixir's.

Ruby testing has historically been dominated by RSpec, but Minitest has made a resurgence in recent years. Minitest is rooted in providing a minimal set of assertions so that tests remain simple. RSpec rooted itself in a more comprehensive assertion library and has many options for setting up data.

Elixir's testing framework—ExUnit—is included with the language. You don't need to install anything to use it. In some languages, the built-in testing framework isn't great, but ExUnit is actually good. (This is evidenced by the fact that there isn't another mainstream testing framework in Elixir.)

ExUnit is similar to Minitest in that it uses a few simple assertions and has minimal options for setting up test cases. This minimal approach has proven to be powerful for ExUnit. It's quick to learn, and you'll often find that you have everything you need to write clean, expressive tests.

Let's dive in!

Test NewMessage Changeset

The first test we're going to write is for an Ecto changeset. This is a great first test to write because the test doesn't involve database or web requests. All that we need to do is call a function and check the output of it.

Let's verify that your environment is correctly set up to run tests. Type `mix test` and verify that your existing tests are green:

```
$ mix test
.....
Finished in 0.08 seconds (0.04s async, 0.04s sync)
5 tests, 0 failures
```

These five tests are the default tests included by Phoenix. You could remove them, but we'll keep them for now and move on.

Your tests should be green without any extra steps. If you do run into an error, it would likely be around the database setup. If this occurs, run `MIX_ENV=test mix do ecto.drop, ecto.create, ecto.migrate` to reset your test database. (You can make an alias for this in `mix.exs`, but it isn't included by default.)

Now let's test the changeset. Create the file test/phone_app/conversations/schema/new_message_test.exs and add the following code:

```
phone_app/test/phone_app/conversations/schema/new_message_test.exs
defmodule PhoneApp.Conversations.Schema.NewMessageTest do
  use ExUnit.Case, async: true

  alias PhoneApp.Conversations.Schema.NewMessage
end
```

Make sure you named the file with the .exs file extension! Many new Elixir developers get tripped up when they name a test file .ex and then it doesn't work.

This sets up a new ExUnit test case. The option async: true makes our tests automatically run in parallel with other test files. This massively speeds up tests across a large codebase. There are times when you wouldn't want to use async tests, but that's outside of the scope of this chapter.

Let's add a test case. We'll test our required fields, that the country code is automatically added, and that the phone number is valid.

phone_app/test/phone_app/conversations/schema/new_message_test.exs

```
Line 1  describe "changeset/1" do
          test "fields are required" do
            cs = NewMessage.changeset(%{})

    5       assert [
              to: {"can't be blank", _}, body: {"can't be blank", _}
            ] = cs.errors
          end

    10      test "the country code is added if not present" do
              assert %{
                errors: [],
                changes: %{to: "+1 5005550006"}
              } = NewMessage.changeset(%{"body" => "test", "to" => "5005550006"})
    15      end

            test "the phone number is validated" do
              assert %{
                errors: [to: {"is an invalid phone number", _}]
              } = NewMessage.changeset(%{"body" => "test", "to" => "+1 111-222-3333"})
    20      end
          end
        end
```

Run mix test to see that your new tests are green. Let's break these tests down in the next section—we'll go line by line to cover how the test works.

Going Through Our Changeset Tests

We wrap everything inside of the describe/2 macro. This isn't required, but it's a best practice to group and name your tests—typically based on the function name. Each test is wrapped inside of the test/2 macro. Everything inside of a test block runs as an individual test case.

Inside of an individual test case, we have access to the same modules and functions available to our application. We don't need to do anything special to access our application's modules—ExUnit includes everything for us automatically. This lets us use the `NewMessage.changeset/1` function on line 3. (An alias at the top makes it more convenient for us to call this function.)

The main test function that you'll use is `assert/1`. This function is small but mighty. You can do simple equality assertions. For example, `assert 1 == 1` is a valid assertion line. But you can also use pattern matching. For example, `assert %{a: _} = %{a: 1}` is a valid assertion.

The power of the pattern assertion style is that ExUnit will show you exactly what diverges when the pattern isn't matched. It's capable of printing this out in an easy-to-read, color-coded format, so you can tell exactly what's different between the left and right sides of the assertion.

All of our tests use pattern assertions to verify that our changeset shape matches an expected value. For example, line 11 asserts that there are no errors in the changeset and that the phone number matches a specific value. Because pattern matching is used, we only need to check for the fields that we care about. (If we were to use equality comparison, then we'd need to exactly match every single field.)

Try changing the assertion pattern so that the test fails. You should see the exact problem highlighted by ExUnit.

These tests are simple. They use functions that don't touch the database or require setup. Let's look at a more complex test case next. You'll see how to test Ecto queries.

What to Test

I don't believe that everything should be tested. There has to be a balance between test value, effort, and business value. That said, I strongly believe in the importance of testing and that you should have a robust test suite for any production application.

Usually, I don't test the framework. In the case of our Ecto schemas, I wouldn't test that our schema has fields or that it operates a certain way. I know these things to be true. I would test that the required fields work correctly and that any validations work correctly because those are implemented by my application.

When in doubt, always test. But don't let testing be the barrier to finishing your feature.

Test an Ecto Query

It's simple to test code that uses database queries. We need to use a special test case that's provided to us by the Phoenix generator. This includes transactional test cases, which means that our test database is cleaned up after each test.

We'll test the ContactStore module because it has functions for retrieving and writing data. We will skip SmsMessageStore because it has many more functions. But the book's provided code (phone_app folder) has tests for the entire application.

Create test/phone_app/conversations/query/contact_store_test.exs and add the following code:

```
phone_app/test/phone_app/conversations/query/contact_store_test.exs
defmodule PhoneApp.Conversations.Query.ContactStoreTest do
  use PhoneApp.DataCase, async: true

  alias PhoneApp.Conversations.Query.ContactStore

  describe "upsert_contact/1" do
    @incoming %{
      from: "111-222-3333",
      to: "999-888-7777",
      direction: :incoming
    }

    @outgoing %{@incoming | direction: :outgoing}

    test "a new contact is created, based on direction" do
      assert {:ok, contact} = ContactStore.upsert_contact(@incoming)
      assert contact.id
      assert contact.phone_number == "111-222-3333"

      assert {:ok, contact2} = ContactStore.upsert_contact(@outgoing)
      assert contact2.id
      assert contact2.id != contact.id
      assert contact2.phone_number == "999-888-7777"
    end

    test "a contact with the same phone number is updated" do
      assert {:ok, contact} = ContactStore.upsert_contact(@incoming)
      assert {:ok, contact2} = ContactStore.upsert_contact(@incoming)

      assert contact2.updated_at != contact.updated_at
      assert Map.delete(contact2, :updated_at) ==
               Map.delete(contact, :updated_at)
    end
  end
end
```

```
35    describe "get_contact!/1" do
        test "no contact raises an error" do
          assert_raise(Ecto.NoResultsError, fn ->
            ContactStore.get_contact!(0)
40        end)
        end

        test "a contact is returned" do
          assert {:ok, contact} = ContactStore.upsert_contact(@incoming)
45        assert ContactStore.get_contact!(contact.id) == contact
        end
      end
    end
```

The use statement on line 2 has changed to PhoneApp.DataCase. This module was created by the Phoenix generator—you can find the module at test/support/data_case.ex. PhoneApp.DataCase is based on ExUnit.Case, but it sets up the PhoneApp.Repo so it can be used in our test module.

These tests largely speak for themselves, but the module attribute on line 7 is new. Test modules are just normal Elixir code! This means we can use module attributes to simplify our testing code. We don't do it here, but we can even define helper functions in our test to extract repeated code.

We use a mix of pattern assertions (line 16) and strict equality assertions (line 18) throughout our test module. However, line 38 introduces the assert_raise/2 assertion. This assertion macro accepts an anonymous function and asserts that a particular error is raised from it.

To demonstrate the importance of tests, these tests revealed a bug in the original Repo.insert/2 function. The fix was to add returning: true to the insert options. If you run into an error with that particular test, make sure that option is used in your Repo.insert/2 call in ContactStore.upsert_contact/1.

Let's test our outbound HTTP requests next.

Test External API Requests

There are many opinions on how to test external requests. Rubyists use mocking (RSpec and Minitest both include mocking capabilities) at the method level or mocking at the HTTP level (VCR) to test external dependencies. Personally, I always reached for VCR because of how simple and powerful it was.

The solution for testing external requests in Elixir is largely the same: mock the function or mock the HTTP request. Personally, I usually mock at the

HTTP request level. The best way to do HTTP mocking in Elixir is with the Bypass library, so let's add that to our project.

Bypass[1] offers a pretty amazing testing capability. Because Elixir is able to spin up multiple applications at once, Bypass takes advantage of this and spins up actual HTTP servers. Instead of mocking the HTTP request at the source, it mocks HTTP requests at the destination! This approach is useful because it tests that your entire HTTP stack works as expected.

Add the Bypass library in your mix.exs file:

```
phone_app/mix.exs
{:bypass, "~> 2.1"}
```

And then run mix deps.get to pull in the dependency. In addition, add the following code to test.exs:

```
phone_app/config/test.exs
config :phone_app, :twilio,
  key_sid: "mock-key-sid",
  key_secret: "mock-key",
  account_sid: "mock-account",
  number: "+19998887777",
  base_url: "http://localhost:4005/2010-04-01"
```

And also create the following JSON file at test/support/fixtures/success.json:

```
phone_app/test/support/fixtures/success.json
{
  "account_sid": "account_sid",
  "sid": "sid",
  "body": "body",
  "from": "+11112223333",
  "to": "+19998887777",
  "status": "sent"
}
```

Now, we can write a test for our API requests. We'll do this by testing the Conversations.send_sms_message/1 function. This test will ensure that our HTTP request works and that it's handled correctly by the send_sms_message/1 function.

Create test/phone_app/conversations/conversations_test.exs and add the following code:

```
phone_app/test/phone_app/conversations/conversations_test.exs
Line 1 defmodule PhoneApp.ConversationsTest do
         use PhoneApp.DataCase, async: true

         alias PhoneApp.Conversations
    5    alias PhoneApp.Conversations.Schema.NewMessage
```

---

1. https://hexdocs.pm/bypass/Bypass.html

```elixir
describe "send_sms_message/1" do
  test "successful request creates an SMS message" do
    bypass = Bypass.open()
    Process.put(:twilio_base_url, "http://localhost:#{bypass.port}")

    resp = Jason.decode!(File.read!("test/support/fixtures/success.json"))

    Bypass.expect_once(
      bypass,
      "POST",
      "/Accounts/mock-account/Messages.json",
      fn conn ->
        conn
        |> Plug.Conn.put_resp_header("Content-Type", "application/json")
        |> Plug.Conn.resp(201, Jason.encode!(resp))
      end
    )

    assert {:ok, message} = Conversations.send_sms_message(%NewMessage{})
    assert message.from == resp["from"]
    assert message.to == resp["to"]
    assert message.body == resp["body"]
    assert message.message_sid == resp["sid"]
    assert message.account_sid == resp["account_sid"]
    assert message.status == resp["status"]
    assert message.direction == :outgoing
  end

  test "a failed request returns an error" do
    bypass = Bypass.open()
    Process.put(:twilio_base_url, "http://localhost:#{bypass.port}")

    Bypass.expect_once(
      bypass,
      "POST",
      "/Accounts/mock-account/Messages.json",
      fn conn ->
        Plug.Conn.resp(conn, 500, "")
      end
    )

    assert Conversations.send_sms_message(%NewMessage{}) ==
             {:error, "Failed to send message"}
  end
end
```

This test is fairly long, but the individual components are not complex. We use the Bypass library by calling Bypass.open/0 on line 9. This creates a testing server endpoint, but it doesn't connect it to our request. Our PhoneApp.Twilio.Api module looks for the :twilio_base_url process dictionary entry. By putting the Bypass URL into the process dictionary (line 10), our API client makes requests to Bypass instead of a real API.

Bypass works by expecting HTTP requests. We use Bypass.expect_once/4 on line 14 to do this. We specify the details of our expected HTTP request and pass a function that will be used to return the HTTP response. In our case, we return a JSON payload (line 21) that's compatible with Twilio's response format.

Based on the response to the Twilio request, our code returns an ok tuple or an error tuple. Our test asserts on both of these cases—line 25 versus line 48. This provides test coverage for our function because it compares both the happy and failure paths.

It may take a while to become comfortable with Bypass. But once you do get comfortable with it, it's incredibly powerful. It's become a critical tool in my personal testing toolbox.

Let's move on to Phoenix endpoint testing next.

Test Phoenix Requests

It's more complex to test endpoints than it is to test pure functions or Ecto queries, but Phoenix provides several helper functions to make it as easy as possible. You'll find more complexity in deciding what to test (complex HTML responses, valid versus invalid parameters, full integration testing versus mock testing, and so on) than you will in writing the actual tests. However, lean toward testing more than less so that you have confidence in your system.

We'll set up the test module and then walk through a few types of controller tests. But first, let's create a little helper to make our tests simpler.

Create Helper Factory

It's common as you write tests to create the same test data over and over again. Usually, setting up data correctly requires multiple lines of code and is susceptible to change as the application develops further. It would be tedious to manually create data again and again, but there's a better way: test factories.

A test factory is a function that initializes data depending on what you need for a particular test. Factories let us set up data without duplicating complex code across our entire application. In our test suite, we're going to use a basic factory function that creates an SMS message.

Create test/support/factory/sms_message.ex and add the following code:

```
phone_app/test/support/factory/sms_message.ex
defmodule Test.Factory.SmsMessageFactory do
  def params(overrides \\ %{}) do
    %{
      from: "+11112223333",
      to: "+19998887777",
      direction: :outgoing,
      message_sid: Ecto.UUID.generate(),
      account_sid: "account_sid",
      body: "body",
      status: "queued"
    }
    |> Map.merge(overrides)
  end

  def create(overrides \\ %{}) do
    {:ok, message} =
      overrides
      |> params()
      |> PhoneApp.Conversations.create_sms_message()

    message
  end
end
```

ExUnit is configured by the Phoenix generator to include code inside of test/support during test execution. This will make the factory available to all of our test files.

There are factory libraries in Elixir, but my personal preference is to not use them. Instead, create factory modules and explicitly set up dependencies as needed.

Set Up Your Test Module

Create test/phone_app_web/controllers/message_controller_test.exs and add the following skeleton:

```
phone_app/test/phone_app_web/controllers/message_controller_test.exs
defmodule PhoneAppWeb.MessageControllerTest do
  use PhoneAppWeb.ConnCase, async: true

  alias Test.Factory.SmsMessageFactory
end
```

This skeleton forms the basis of our controller test. We use PhoneAppWeb.ConnCase this time. You'll find that module at test/support/conn_case.ex. The ConnCase module is created by Phoenix and sets up a conn dependency as well as the same dependencies as DataCase.

Test Redirection

Our first test will be for the request GET /messages. We want to ensure that the request is redirected based on whether there's an existing conversation or not. Add the following describe block to your test module:

phone_app/test/phone_app_web/controllers/message_controller_test.exs
```
describe "GET /messages" do
  test "empty messages redirects to new message", %{conn: conn} do
    conn = get(conn, ~p"/messages")
    assert redirected_to(conn, 302) == "/messages/new"
  end

  test "redirects to latest messages", %{conn: conn} do
    _m1 = SmsMessageFactory.create(%{to: "111-222-3333", body: "Test 1"})
    m2 = SmsMessageFactory.create(%{to: "211-222-3333", body: "Test 2"})

    conn = get(conn, ~p"/messages")
    assert redirected_to(conn, 302) == "/messages/#{m2.contact_id}"
  end
end
```

The second argument of each test block—%{conn: conn}—takes the conn set up by ConnCase and injects it into the test block. We pass the conn variable into the get/2 function along with the route that we want to run against. The endpoint is then executed, and the conn variable is transformed based on the output of the request.

In this test, we use the redirected_to/2 function to assert that our requests are correctly redirected. We use our SMS factory to set up the data used in our test.

Test HTML Responses

Our next test will be for the request GET /messages/new. This controller returns HTML containing a form, so we want to make sure that's being returned correctly. Add the following describe block to your test module:

phone_app/test/phone_app_web/controllers/message_controller_test.exs
```
describe "GET /messages/new" do
  test "a message form is rendered", %{conn: conn} do
    conn = get(conn, ~p"/messages/new")

    assert html = html_response(conn, 200)
    assert html =~ ~S(<form action="/messages/new" method="post")
    assert html =~ "Send a message..."
    assert html =~ "To (Phone Number)"
  end
end
```

This test uses html_response/2 to prove that a 200 status is returned along with an HTML body. The HTML is returned as a string, so we use regular expressions to test against it.

Each line like assert html =~ "a string" proves that the HTML code is inside of the response body. It's a good practice to test only the key elements on your page. If you test too many elements, then your test can become brittle. Brittle tests are painful over time because updates can break unrelated tests.

Test Post Requests

Phoenix makes it just as easy to test POST requests as it is to test GET requests. However, our test will be slightly more complex due to how our endpoint works.

Our endpoint makes an outbound HTTP request to Twilio, so we need to use Bypass to set up our test. Add the following describe block to your test module:

phone_app/test/phone_app_web/controllers/message_controller_test.exs

```
Line 1  alias PhoneApp.Conversations.Schema.SmsMessage

        describe "POST /messages/new" do
          test "invalid params is rejected", %{conn: conn} do
     5      conn = post(conn, ~p"/messages/new", %{})
            assert html_response(conn, 200) =~
                     Plug.HTML.html_escape("can't be blank")
          end

    10    test "valid params creates a message", %{conn: conn} do
            bypass = Bypass.open()
            Process.put(:twilio_base_url, "http://localhost:#{bypass.port}")

            Bypass.expect_once(
    15        bypass,
              "POST",
              "/Accounts/mock-account/Messages.json",
              fn conn ->
                conn
    20          |> put_resp_header("Content-Type", "application/json")
                |> resp(201, File.read!("test/support/fixtures/success.json"))
              end
            )

    25      params = %{message: %{to: "+1111-222-3333", body: "Test"}}
            conn = post(conn, ~p"/messages/new", params)
            assert redirected_to(conn, 302) == "/messages"
            assert PhoneApp.Repo.aggregate(SmsMessage, :count) == 1
          end
    30  end
```

This test is comparable to our previous tests, but it uses post/3 (lines 5 and 26) instead of get/2. We pass our data payload as the third argument to post/3. It's important to test both happy and failure cases, so our tests include examples for both.

Notice the use of Plug.HTML.html_escape/1 in our HTML assertion on line 7. Phoenix will automatically escape HTML entities such as single quotation marks, so our test also needs to escape single quotation marks. If we didn't escape the assertion, then you'd get a failed test.

Now that we've tested our Phoenix requests, it's time to turn our attention to Oban.

Test Oban Jobs

You'll often want to test two different things with Oban: that jobs are enqueued properly and that jobs work as expected. Oban provides test helpers for each of these situations. We'll first test that our StatusWorker job is enqueued when an outgoing SMS message is created.

Test Jobs Are Enqueued

When we create an SMS message in the PhoneApp.Conversations module, we conditionally create an Oban job based on whether the SMS message is outgoing or not. So, we need to test that certain SMS messages enqueue the StatusWorker job, but other SMS messages don't enqueue a job.

We'll use the Oban.Testing module[2] to verify that the create_sms_message/1 function works correctly.

Add the following code to the existing ConversationsTest module:

phone_app/test/phone_app/conversations/conversations_test.exs
```
Line 1  use Oban.Testing, repo: Repo

     -  alias PhoneApp.Conversations.Worker.StatusWorker

     5  describe "create_sms_message/1" do
     -    test "a valid SMS message is created" do
     -      params = Test.Factory.SmsMessageFactory.params()
     -      assert {:ok, msg} = Conversations.create_sms_message(params)
     -      assert_enqueued(worker: StatusWorker, args: %{"id" => msg.id})
    10    end

     -    test "incoming SMS message doesn't enqueue a worker" do
     -      params = Test.Factory.SmsMessageFactory.params(%{direction: :incoming})
     -      assert {:ok, _msg} = Conversations.create_sms_message(params)
```

---

2. https://hexdocs.pm/oban/Oban.Testing.html

```
15      refute_enqueued(worker: StatusWorker)
   -  end

   -  test "an invalid message returns an error" do
   -    params = Test.Factory.SmsMessageFactory.params(%{message_sid: ""})
20     assert {:error, _} = Conversations.create_sms_message(params)
   -    refute_enqueued(worker: StatusWorker)
   -  end
   - end
```

We are able to use the Oban test functions because Oban is configured to manual testing mode (you updated config/text.exs in Add Oban to Our SMS App, on page 161). The assert_enqueued (line 9) and refute_enqueued (lines 15 and 21) functions are used to test whether a particular job is enqueued or not.

The arguments to the testing functions are optional, but they provide scoping to the particular job you're targeting. This is important because you don't want your tests to fail as more job types are introduced to your application.

Test Job Implementation

In the previous section, we covered job creation. But we still need to test that the job works correctly.

Our next test will cover the StatusWorker module. You can take different approaches for testing Oban workers. Oban offers a perform_job/3 helper function, but it's often not needed. A worker is just a module that implements the perform/1 function, so we can call that function directly. We'll use this simple approach for our test.

Create test/phone_app/conversations/worker/status_worker_test.exs and add the following code:

phone_app/test/phone_app/conversations/worker/status_worker_test.exs
```
Line 1  defmodule PhoneApp.Conversations.Worker.StatusWorkerTest do
   -    use PhoneApp.DataCase, async: true

   -    alias PhoneApp.Conversations.Worker.StatusWorker
5       alias Test.Factory.SmsMessageFactory

   -    defp setup_bypass(message, status: status) do
   -      bypass = Bypass.open()
   -      Process.put(:twilio_base_url, "http://localhost:#{bypass.port}")
10
   -      Bypass.expect_once(
   -        bypass,
   -        "GET",
   -        "/Accounts/account_sid/Messages/#{message.message_sid}.json",
```

```elixir
15        fn conn ->
            conn
            |> Plug.Conn.put_resp_header("Content-Type", "application/json")
            |> Plug.Conn.resp(200, Jason.encode!(%{status: status}))
          end
20      )
      end

      test "a message status is updated" do
        message = SmsMessageFactory.create()
25      setup_bypass(message, status: "delivered")

        assert {:ok, job} = StatusWorker.enqueue(message)
        assert {:ok, updated} = StatusWorker.perform(job)

30      assert updated.status == "delivered"
        assert Repo.reload(message) == updated
      end

      test "not ready yet, enqueue" do
35      message = SmsMessageFactory.create()
        setup_bypass(message, status: "queued")

        assert {:ok, job} = StatusWorker.enqueue(message)
        assert StatusWorker.perform(job) == {:error, "Message not ready"}
40      assert Repo.reload(message) == message
      end
    end
```

We use Bypass in our test to mock out several scenarios. It takes a few lines of code to set up Bypass, so the setup_bypass/2 function on line 7 handles this for us. Because of it, our test functions are easier to read.

Our test first enqueues a job (line 27) using the StatusWorker.enqueue/1 function. Then, the job is performed (line 28) and the expected result is asserted. Our test ensures that both enqueue/1 and perform/1 work. We repeat this process on line 38 to prove that the different logic paths in our worker are correct.

With that, we have a tested StatusWorker module! All of the different components of our application have tests too. There's a lot more that could be taught about testing, but this is a solid foundation for you to test your applications.

Wrapping Up

Tests are critical for production applications. They give you confidence that your application works as expected and will handle errors correctly. The way that you test doesn't matter as much as having the tests, so start early!

Elixir provides a built-in testing framework called ExUnit. It's a great testing library that has an intentionally limited number of features and assertions. Despite being a small library, ExUnit is powerful and expressive—largely due to its support for pattern matching. ExUnit verifies that asserted patterns match correctly. And if a pattern doesn't match, ExUnit highlights what specifically was different between the left and right sides.

ExUnit tests are specified by using the ExUnit.Case module. This brings in all of the testing functions so you have complete access to test your code. Otherwise, ExUnit test modules are just plain modules. You can create private functions and module attributes to create clean tests. Plus, you can use test-only modules like testing factories to streamline your tests.

Phoenix provides the DataCase and ConnCase modules to enable the testing of queries and endpoints. Other libraries, like Oban, provide their own testing helpers to make it easy to test your application code. Sometimes your tests get complex though, such as when testing external API requests. Bypass solves testing external API requests by spinning up short-lived HTTP servers that are used by your test suite.

That's it for our application! But there's still one more chapter. We'll cover developing and advanced libraries in Elixir that show a strong future for the Elixir ecosystem.

## CHAPTER 11

The Future of Elixir

This book is coming to an end, but your Elixir journey is just starting. There's so much more to see and learn about Elixir! In the past few years, major advancements have come to the Elixir ecosystem that push many exciting new use cases for Elixir. In addition to these exciting advancements, there are useful topics for you to dive into after you finish this book.

It's important to see forward progress in languages that you use—otherwise, things feel stale. If you look at Ruby, a lot of exciting advances have been made in the past few years, such as new real-time capabilities, improvements to developer experience, consolidation of libraries into Rails core, and increased performance. Luckily, Elixir has also been developing at an amazing speed.

We'll look at the projects that are making up the future of Elixir: LiveView, machine learning with Nx, and development toward a type system. But before we cover those, there are a few key topics that are good to know about. We'll briefly cover deployment, observability, real-time apps, and GraphQL.

This chapter provides an intro to each topic—it's a jumping off point for areas that you're interested in. Be sure to make a mental note of the topics you want to explore in more detail later.

Let's kick it off by looking at deployment and observability.

Deployment and Observability

Building the first version of an app is just step one in getting users to use it. You need to deploy it to production, know that it's working properly, market it, support users, and so much more. This book won't help you with marketing or supporting an app, but it will help with deployment and observability!

Elixir has had fairly large advances in deployment patterns over the last few years. In 2019,[1] the concept of Mix releases was made available. We'll walk through the benefits of releases and how you can use them. After that, we'll cover a few options for observing your app.

Deploy an Elixir App

You could bundle up your application and run it in production using mix phx.server. But there's a better option that will reduce long-term friction— Mix releases.[2]

A release is a self-contained package that bundles your compiled code alongside the Erlang VM and runtime. It provides benefits such as code preloading, more configuration options, and not requiring source code in production. It also includes management scripts that make it possible to do things like connect to a running application.

Phoenix has a deployment guide[3] that walks you through deploying an application using Mix releases. We won't walk through the guide here, but this is the best way to deploy your first app. It even includes a Dockerfile that you can use to spin up a containerized version of your application on AWS, GCP, Fly.io, Render, or other cloud providers.

Once you have your app running in production, you need to know if it's working properly.

Observe Your Production Apps

Observability is the art of monitoring your application so that you know what's good and bad with it. There are many different types of observability. Application logging, bug reporting, backend performance monitoring, and frontend tracking are all examples of observability.

The Telemetry[4] library serves as the modern foundation for collecting observability metrics. Telemetry allows libraries like Phoenix, Ecto, and Oban to provide you with metrics about performance. Each of these libraries emits Telemetry events that can be consumed by your Telemetry handlers. The entire system is standardized, so your handlers and a library's events work on top of the same foundation.

---

1.   https://elixir-lang.org/blog/2019/06/24/elixir-v1-9-0-released/
2.   https://hexdocs.pm/mix/Mix.Tasks.Release.html
3.   https://hexdocs.pm/phoenix/releases.html
4.   https://hexdocs.pm/telemetry/readme.html

You can use Telemetry events to write to StatsD reporters such as Datadog, or you can write your own custom handlers. Plus, due to standardization, you can usually integrate a new library's Telemetry events quickly into your existing handlers.

Phoenix provides an in-depth guide[5] on how to use Telemetry events to monitor your application that uses Phoenix. Many other libraries include similar documentation on their telemetry events.

Telemetry is just one type of observability. Another big one is backend performance monitoring. Most of the major players like New Relic and Scout APM support Elixir and provide guides on how to integrate it. This also applies for bug-tracking platforms like Bugsnag, Rollbar, and Sentry.

The most important thing about observability is to do it early. You don't want to have a production problem and not be aware of it or not be able to diagnose the cause of it.

Let's change gears and look at how LiveView is powering the future of real-time apps in Elixir.

Real-Time Apps with LiveView

Elixir has a solid foundation in real-time application development. It started with Phoenix Channels, which I wrote all about in *Real-Time Phoenix [Bus20]*. But there's been an awesome library that has completely dominated real-time application development in Elixir—LiveView. (It's so popular that it's often the first thing people hear about Elixir.)

LiveView[6] is a library that enables a new breed of real-time applications. It is server-centric, which means that all of the page HTML is processed on the server and efficiently sent to clients on update. So, if a change happens on the server, connected clients are instantly and automatically updated.

The magic of LiveView is that it enables you to create powerful applications with minimal JavaScript. All of the page interactions are processed by the LiveView process, so the server stays in control of the page interactions. In my experience, the amount of JavaScript needed to create a single-page app experience is reduced by 95% or more!

LiveView was briefly mentioned in Chapter 7, Serving Requests with Phoenix, on page 117, but it's so prevalent in the Elixir ecosystem that it deserves its

---

5. https://hexdocs.pm/phoenix/telemetry.html
6. https://hexdocs.pm/phoenix_live_view/welcome.html

own spot in this chapter. Make sure to check out *Programming Phoenix LiveView [TD24]* by Bruce Tate and Sophie DeBenedetto. It's the best book to get started with LiveView!

If you're building a LiveView app, you likely won't have a traditional HTTP-based API. But if you're not using LiveView, consider using GraphQL. Let's talk about that next.

GraphQL with Absinthe

GraphQL is a popular technology to build APIs with. It replaces traditional REST-based APIs with a completely different approach to API development. It can be a bit complex to get started with, but it's a fast and effective approach for API development. If you do decide to build a GraphQL API, the quality of your server implementation is important. Luckily, Elixir has one of the best implementations out there.

Absinthe[7] is the leading server implementation of GraphQL in Elixir. It provides all of the basics that you'd expect but also includes more advanced features such as subscriptions, full middleware control, and Relay support.

One of the hardest things to get right with a GraphQL API is batched resolution—you want to grab the data you need in the fewest number of queries possible. Absinthe has multiple approaches to solving this problem—arguably in a better way than other languages provide.

GraphQL is a paradigm shift from traditional ways of building APIs, but in my experience, it's worth it. The book *Craft GraphQL APIs in Elixir with Absinthe [WW18]* by Bruce Williams and Ben Wilson walks you through how to build your GraphQL with Absinthe, directly from the creators of the Absinthe framework.

Machine Learning with Nx and Bumblebee

Machine learning and artificial intelligence have been hot topics in recent years. Python is the most important language in the machine learning community, but Elixir is working on becoming a contender. Machine learning is vastly different than classical programming though, and it requires new ways of executing code.

Nx (Numerical Elixir)[8] was developed by Sean Moriarity and José Valim to solve the problem of machine learning in Elixir. Nx provides primitives that

---

7. https://hexdocs.pm/absinthe/overview.html
8. https://hexdocs.pm/nx/Nx.html

enable code to run on computing targets such as GPUs. Nx is a low-level library that's leveraged by higher-level libraries to implement common machine learning patterns.

Bumblebee[9] is a library that leverages Nx to execute pretrained neural network models. It works out of the box with HuggingFace models, which is the most popular host for machine learning models. Bumblebee has been shown to work with popular models such as "Whisper" and "Stable Diffusion."

Livebook[10] isn't strictly machine learning related, but it's commonly used in a similar way to Jupyter notebooks, which are used in the Python community to share executable code alongside the results of the code. Livebook executes Elixir code located in cells and creates a formatted, documented notebook of code that can be shared between team members.

The development of machine learning capabilities in Elixir is incredibly exciting. Elixir's capabilities with robust data pipelines and distributed code execution make it a perfect contender in the machine learning space because of the amount of work that goes into bringing machine learning models to production. However, there's still a lot of work to do in this space. Keep an eye on it because it has shown so much promise so far.

For our final topic, let's look at potential type system support in Elixir.

Type Systems

For better or worse, one of the most commonly asked questions by developers coming from another language is whether Elixir provides types support. The common argument is that static types defined in an application allow for more predictability and guarantees about how an application will perform. (Whether those claims are true or not is a matter of opinion.)

Many Elixirists take advantage of pattern matching and structs to achieve a loose version of typing. If you use a struct match like message = %SmsMessage{} in your function head, then you know that message will be an SmsMessage. This actually goes a long way, but it's not a true types support.

Dialyzer is an Erlang package that provides a "success typing" implementation for BEAM languages. There is an Elixir library that wraps it called Dialyxir.[11] This package can catch a lot of logic mistakes in your code, but it's not native

---

9.   https://github.com/elixir-nx/bumblebee
10. https://livebook.dev/
11. https://github.com/jeremyjh/dialyxir

to the Elixir compiler. Plus, it can have problems with accuracy and speed. It's recommended that you use Dialyzer, but it's not a true types support either.

Dialyzer uses a concept called Typespecs[12] to define types—in addition to what it can automatically determine from your code. You may see @spec definitions in Elixir codebases that you work on. They look like this:

```
# Example from Typespecs docs
@spec long_word?(word()) :: boolean()
def long_word?(word) when is_binary(word) do
  String.length(word) > 8
end
```

Typespecs are used for documentation and by tools like Dialyzer, but there may be more uses for them in the future.

José Valim opened the discussion for a real type system in Elixir with a blog post[13] and presentation at ElixirConf 2022. The team has enlisted the help of PhD researchers to develop an Elixir type system based on set-theoretic types. This is big news because it was largely considered impossible to add true types support to Erlang and Elixir.

There's no guarantee that this research will result in a types implementation. It will only be added if it's performant, accurate, and easy to use. As of January 2024, José tweeted[14] that "Elixir is, officially, a gradually typed language." So the future is bright, and the community is hoping to see a true types system in Elixir one day!

Wrapping Up

Your Elixir toolbox has quite a few tools in it, but it's nowhere near complete yet. There's so much to learn, and there are different paths that you can take based on your interests. This is a good thing though because it means you can expand your knowledge and interests over time.

The first thing you'll need to do once you write your first Elixir app is deploy it somewhere. Use Mix releases to create your release and package it up into a container. You'll be able to easily deploy to platforms like AWS, GCP, Fly.io, or Render. Once your application is deployed, make sure that you have proper observability in place, such as application logging, performance monitoring, and bug tracking.

---

12. https://hexdocs.pm/elixir/typespecs.html
13. https://elixir-lang.org/blog/2022/10/05/my-future-with-elixir-set-theoretic-types/
14. https://twitter.com/josevalim/status/1744395345872683471

If you're looking for a different way to build applications, then Phoenix LiveView may be the library for you. LiveView enables you to create real-time, rich user interfaces with a minimal amount of JavaScript. When you create a LiveView app, your code executes on the server, so you can stick to Elixir for most of your application development. Cut 95% or more of your application's JavaScript with LiveView!

LiveView isn't for you? Then consider GraphQL to build your application APIs. Absinthe is an implementation of GraphQL that provides all of the bells and whistles you need. It's arguably one of the better GraphQL implementations, and it even comes with subscriptions, Relay, and batch resolution support.

Machine learning and AI are coming to Elixir. The Nx project provides a foundation for numerical computing in Elixir. With Nx, you can target code to run on GPUs—which is crucial for machine learning applications. Bumblebee lets you run pretrained models with ease. Spin up the hottest machine learning models in minutes, all without touching Python.

Finally, keep an eye out for type system development in Elixir. Nothing is guaranteed, but there have been discussions of innovative type system approaches that may finally bring types support to Elixir. But if those developments don't come to fruition, we still have the Dialyzer library to provide types to our Elixir apps.

The future of Elixir is bright!

The End of Our Journey

It's the end of this book, but it's just the beginning of your Elixir journey. Thank you for letting me guide you as you took your first steps with Elixir!

The feeling I had when I first learned Elixir was that it would dramatically change how I program—and it did. Not only did my Elixir skills improve over time, but I also found that my system design as a whole dramatically improved as well. I know that learning Elixir will positively affect how you build systems, too.

The Elixir ecosystem is continuing to grow—thanks to developers like yourself who are curious about it. The Elixir community is very welcoming, so please never feel alone as you continue your Elixir journey. Join one of the branches of the community (forums, Slack, Discord, and more) and let us give you a hand!

Now, go forth and build awesome Elixir applications.

Bibliography

[Bus20]   Stephen Bussey. *Real-Time Phoenix*. The Pragmatic Bookshelf, Dallas, TX, 2020.

[LM21]   Andrea Leopardi and Jeffrey Matthias. *Testing Elixir*. The Pragmatic Bookshelf, Dallas, TX, 2021.

[McC15]   Chris McCord. *Metaprogramming Elixir*. The Pragmatic Bookshelf, Dallas, TX, 2015.

[TD24]   Bruce A. Tate and Sophie DeBenedetto. *Programming Phoenix LiveView*. The Pragmatic Bookshelf, Dallas, TX, 2024.

[TV19]   Chris McCord, Bruce Tate and José Valim. *Programming Phoenix 1.4*. The Pragmatic Bookshelf, Dallas, TX, 2019.

[WM19]   Darin Wilson and Eric Meadows-Jönsson. *Programming Ecto*. The Pragmatic Bookshelf, Dallas, TX, 2019.

[WW18]   Bruce Williams and Ben Wilson. *Craft GraphQL APIs in Elixir with Absinthe*. The Pragmatic Bookshelf, Dallas, TX, 2018.

Index

Thank you!

We hope you enjoyed this book and that you're already thinking about what you want to learn next. To help make that decision easier, we're offering you this gift.

Head on over to https://pragprog.com right now, and use the coupon code BUYANOTHER2024 to save 30% on your next ebook. Offer is void where prohibited or restricted. This offer does not apply to any edition of *The Pragmatic Programmer* ebook.

And if you'd like to share your own expertise with the world, why not propose a writing idea to us? After all, many of our best authors started off as our readers, just like you. With up to a 50% royalty, world-class editorial services, and a name you trust, there's nothing to lose. Visit https://pragprog.com/become-an-author/ today to learn more and to get started.

Thank you for your continued support. We hope to hear from you again soon!

The Pragmatic Bookshelf

Real-Time Phoenix

Give users the real-time experience they expect, by using Elixir and Phoenix Channels to build applications that instantly react to changes and reflect the application's true state. Learn how Elixir and Phoenix make it easy and enjoyable to create real-time applications that scale to a large number of users. Apply system design and development best practices to create applications that are easy to maintain. Gain confidence by learning how to break your applications before your users do. Deploy applications with minimized resource use and maximized performance.

Stephen Bussey
(326 pages) ISBN: 9781680507195. $45.95
https://pragprog.com/book/sbsockets

Adopting Elixir

Adoption is more than programming. Elixir is an exciting new language, but to successfully get your application from start to finish, you're going to need to know more than just the language. You need the case studies and strategies in this book. Learn the best practices for the whole life of your application, from design and team-building, to managing stakeholders, to deployment and monitoring. Go beyond the syntax and the tools to learn the techniques you need to develop your Elixir application from concept to production.

Ben Marx, José Valim, Bruce Tate
(242 pages) ISBN: 9781680502527. $42.95
https://pragprog.com/book/tvmelixir

Functional Web Development with Elixir, OTP, and Phoenix

Elixir and Phoenix are generating tremendous excitement as an unbeatable platform for building modern web applications. For decades OTP has helped developers create incredibly robust, scalable applications with unparalleled uptime. Make the most of them as you build a stateful web app with Elixir, OTP, and Phoenix. Model domain entities without an ORM or a database. Manage server state and keep your code clean with OTP Behaviours. Layer on a Phoenix web interface without coupling it to the business logic. Open doors to powerful new techniques that will get you thinking about web development in fundamentally new ways.

Lance Halvorsen
(218 pages) ISBN: 9781680502435. $45.95
https://pragprog.com/book/lhelph

Metaprogramming Elixir

Write code that writes code with Elixir macros. Macros make metaprogramming possible and define the language itself. In this book, you'll learn how to use macros to extend the language with fast, maintainable code and share functionality in ways you never thought possible. You'll discover how to extend Elixir with your own first-class features, optimize performance, and create domain-specific languages.

Chris McCord
(128 pages) ISBN: 9781680500417. $17
https://pragprog.com/book/cmelixir

Designing Elixir Systems with OTP

You know how to code in Elixir; now learn to think in it. Learn to design libraries with intelligent layers that shape the right data structures, flow from one function into the next, and present the right APIs. Embrace the same OTP that's kept our telephone systems reliable and fast for over 30 years. Move beyond understanding the OTP functions to knowing what's happening under the hood, and why that matters. Using that knowledge, instinctively know how to design systems that deliver fast and resilient services to your users, all with an Elixir focus.

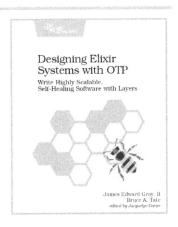

James Edward Gray, II and Bruce A. Tate
(246 pages) ISBN: 9781680506617. $41.95
https://pragprog.com/book/jgotp

Programming Elixir 1.6

This book is *the* introduction to Elixir for experienced programmers, completely updated for Elixir 1.6 and beyond. Explore functional programming without the academic overtones (tell me about monads just one more time). Create concurrent applications, but get them right without all the locking and consistency headaches. Meet Elixir, a modern, functional, concurrent language built on the rock-solid Erlang VM. Elixir's pragmatic syntax and built-in support for metaprogramming will make you productive and keep you interested for the long haul. Maybe the time is right for the Next Big Thing. Maybe it's Elixir.

Dave Thomas
(410 pages) ISBN: 9781680502992. $47.95
https://pragprog.com/book/elixir16

Build a Binary Clock with Elixir and Nerves

Want to get better at coding Elixir? Write a hardware project with Nerves. As you build this binary clock, you'll build in resiliency using OTP, the same libraries powering many commercial phone switches. You'll attack complexity the way the experts do, using a layered approach. You'll sharpen your debugging skills by taking small, easily verified steps toward your goal. When you're done, you'll have a working binary clock and a good appreciation of the work that goes into a hardware system. You'll also be able to apply that understanding to every new line of Elixir you write.

Frank Hunleth and Bruce A. Tate
(106 pages) ISBN: 9781680509236. $29.95
https://pragprog.com/book/thnerves

Build a Weather Station with Elixir and Nerves

The Elixir programming language has become a go-to tool for creating reliable, fault-tolerant, and robust server-side applications. Thanks to Nerves, those same exact benefits can be realized in embedded applications. This book will teach you how to structure, build, and deploy production grade Nerves applications to network-enabled devices. The weather station sensor hub project that you will be embarking upon will show you how to create a full stack IoT solution in record time. You will build everything from the embedded Nerves device to the Phoenix backend and even the Grafana time-series data visualizations.

Alexander Koutmos, Bruce A. Tate, Frank Hunleth
(90 pages) ISBN: 9781680509021. $26.95
https://pragprog.com/book/passweather

Programming Phoenix 1.4

Don't accept the compromise between fast and beautiful: you can have it all. Phoenix creator Chris McCord, Elixir creator José Valim, and award-winning author Bruce Tate walk you through building an application that's fast and reliable. At every step, you'll learn from the Phoenix creators not just what to do, but why. Packed with insider insights and completely updated for Phoenix 1.4, this definitive guide will be your constant companion in your journey from Phoenix novice to expert as you build the next generation of web applications.

Chris McCord, Bruce Tate and José Valim
(356 pages) ISBN: 9781680502268. $45.95
https://pragprog.com/book/phoenix14

Programming Ecto

Languages may come and go, but the relational database endures. Learn how to use Ecto, the premier database library for Elixir, to connect your Elixir and Phoenix apps to databases. Get a firm handle on Ecto fundamentals with a module-by-module tour of the critical parts of Ecto. Then move on to more advanced topics and advice on best practices with a series of recipes that provide clear, step-by-step instructions on scenarios commonly encountered by app developers. Co-authored by the creator of Ecto, this title provides all the essentials you need to use Ecto effectively.

Darin Wilson and Eric Meadows-Jönsson
(242 pages) ISBN: 9781680502824. $45.95
https://pragprog.com/book/wmecto

The Pragmatic Bookshelf

The Pragmatic Bookshelf features books written by professional developers for professional developers. The titles continue the well-known Pragmatic Programmer style and continue to garner awards and rave reviews. As development gets more and more difficult, the Pragmatic Programmers will be there with more titles and products to help you stay on top of your game.

Visit Us Online

This Book's Home Page
https://pragprog.com/book/sbelixir
Source code from this book, errata, and other resources. Come give us feedback, too!

Keep Up-to-Date
https://pragprog.com
Join our announcement mailing list (low volume) or follow us on Twitter @pragprog for new titles, sales, coupons, hot tips, and more.

New and Noteworthy
https://pragprog.com/news
Check out the latest Pragmatic developments, new titles, and other offerings.

Save on the ebook

Save on the ebook versions of this title. Owning the paper version of this book entitles you to purchase the electronic versions at a terrific discount.

PDFs are great for carrying around on your laptop—they are hyperlinked, have color, and are fully searchable. Most titles are also available for the iPhone and iPod touch, Amazon Kindle, and other popular e-book readers.

Send a copy of your receipt to support@pragprog.com and we'll provide you with a discount coupon.

Contact Us

Online Orders:	*https://pragprog.com/catalog*
Customer Service:	*support@pragprog.com*
International Rights:	*translations@pragprog.com*
Academic Use:	*academic@pragprog.com*
Write for Us:	*http://write-for-us.pragprog.com*